HOW'S ʇ

A Little Book on Cricket ƒ

by

H. M. HERMAN
(Master at Dulwich College Preparatory School)

Foreword by
Sir PELHAM WARNER

Introduction by
TREVOR WIGNALL

Copyright © 2013 Read Books Ltd.
This book is copyright and may not be
reproduced or copied in any way without
the express permission of the publisher in writing

British Library Cataloguing-in-Publication Data
A catalogue record for this book is available from the
British Library

A Short History of Cricket

Cricket is a bat-and-ball game played between two teams of eleven players each, on a field at the centre of which is a rectangular twenty-two-yard long pitch. Each team takes its turn to bat, attempting to score runs, while the other team fields. Each turn is known as an innings. Whilst this may sound reasonably simple – the game of cricket has a very long and varied history; changing with time and geographical location.

Early cricket was at some time or other described as 'a club striking a ball (like) the ancient games of club-ball, stool-ball, trap-ball or stob-ball.' The sport can definitely be traced back to Tudor times in early sixteenth century England though. Further written evidence exists of a game known as 'creag' being played by Prince Edward, the son of Edward I, at Newenden, Kent, in 1301. There has been speculation, but no distinct evidence that this was a form of early English cricket.

The earliest definite reference to cricket being played in England (and hence anywhere) is given at a 1598 court case which mentions that 'creckett' was played on common land in Guildford, Surrey around 1550. Here, the court coroner gave witness that 'hee and diverse of his fellows did runne and play [on the common land] at creckett and other plaies.' It is believed that it was originally a children's game but references around 1610 indicate that adults had started playing it and the earliest reference to inter-parish or **village cricket** occurs soon afterwards. In 1624, a player called **Jasper Vinall** was killed when he was struck on the head during a match between two parish teams in Sussex.

During the seventeenth century, numerous references indicate the growth of cricket in the south-east of England. By the end of the century it had become an organised activity being played for high stakes, and it is believed that the first professionals appeared in the years following the Restoration in 1660. The game underwent major development in the eighteenth century and became the national sport of England. Betting played a major part in that development with rich patrons forming their own 'select XIs'. Bowling only really evolved in 1760 though, when bowlers began to pitch the ball instead of rolling or skimming it towards the batsman. This caused a revolution in bat design because to deal with the bouncing ball, it was necessary to introduce the modern straight bat in place of the old 'hockey stick' shape. The nineteenth century saw **underarm bowling** replaced by first **roundarm** and then **overarm bowling**. Both developments were controversial.

Meanwhile, the British Empire had been instrumental in spreading the game overseas, and by the middle of the nineteenth century it had become well established in India, North America, the Caribbean, South Africa, Australia and New Zealand. In 1844, the **first international cricket match** took place between the **United States** and **Canada** (although neither has ever been ranked as a Test-playing nation. In 1862, an English team made the first tour of Australia and in 1876–77, an England team took part in the first-ever **Test match** at the **Melbourne Cricket Ground** against **Australia**. The resultant rivalry gave birth to 'The Ashes' in 1882, and this has remained Test cricket's most famous contest ever since.

The last two decades before the First World War have been called the 'Golden Age of Cricket' – a form of nostalgia in the face of mounting modernisation and destruction. It was (and is) a unique game where in addition to the laws of play, the sportsmen must abide by the 'Spirit of the Game.' The standard of sportsmanship has historically been considered so high that the phrase 'it's just not cricket' was coined in the nineteenth century to describe unfair or underhanded behaviour in any walk of life. In the last few decades though, cricket has become increasingly fast-paced and competitive, increasing the use of appealing and **sledging**, although players are still expected to abide by the umpires' rulings without argument, and for the most part they do.

Cricket entered a new era in 1963 when English counties introduced the **limited overs** variant. As it was sure to produce a result, limited overs cricket was lucrative and the number of matches increased. In the twenty-first century, a new limited overs form, **Twenty20**, has made an immediate impact; though its longevity is yet to be established. As is evident from this brief history of Cricket, it is a sport with a long and fascinating history which has firmly retained its popularity into the present day. We hope the reader is encouraged to find out more and maybe have a game of their own.

[Central Press

"THE TRAGEDY OF THE CROSS BAT"
NOTE.—Even the best of them slip up sometimes

Frontispiece]

CONTENTS

	PAGE
FOREWORD	13
INTRODUCTION	15
THE TOSS	19
FIRST WICKET. BATTING "POSITION," "STANCE," KIT	21
SECOND WICKET. "STILL BATTING" — "THE STROKES"	31
THIRD WICKET. "BOWLING" . . .	48
FOURTH WICKET. BOWLING: ON AGAIN .	60
FIFTH WICKET. FIELDING: LOTS OF IT .	71
SIXTH WICKET. KEEPING WICKET . .	86
SEVENTH WICKET. CAPTAINCY . . .	96
EIGHTH WICKET. PRACTICE AND HOW TO LIVE	106
NINTH WICKET. CRICKET VOCABULARY, ETC.	113
TENTH WICKET. A FEW YARNS . . .	137
EXTRAS	155
CLOSE OF PLAY	158

LIST OF ILLUSTRATIONS

Sketches by
THORPE DIXON

	PAGE
"Wait for it"	23
"Forward defence"	27
"As the bowler's arm comes round"	33
"Just what the bowler wanted"	39
"Got it!"	43
"Just coming over"	55
"A good grip"	60
"Just before a leg-break"	63
Diagram of fielding positions	73
"Slips"	79
Diagram of batsman's shots	83
Listen to your Captain!	99
Fielding—an all-time job	103
Right	115
Wrong	117
Forward defence	119
"Finish of an on-drive"	123

LIST OF PLATES

"The tragedy of the cross bat"	*Frontispiece*
	Facing page
Hobbs cutting	40
"Endeavour"	41
"Zaaaaat"	80
Hammond just gets home	81
Aubrey Smith batting	120
Hammond's off-drive	121

FOREWORD

Mr. H. M. Herman has written a book which should make a ready appeal to all young cricketers, and not only to the young, because, however great a cricketer may be, he learns something new about the Game every day.

The make-up of the book is clear and attractive, and the different points are set out in a vivid and clearly defined manner.

Mr. Herman emphasizes his remarks by references to various distinguished cricketers, and, although there is a plethora of books on Cricket in these days, Mr. Herman's should have a wide public.

I should like to recommend the book to all who are interested in the incomparable Game.

Sir PELHAM WARNER.

INTRODUCTION

As one who does not pretend to be even a semi-authority on cricket but who in the course of his work has written tens of thousands of words about the game, it was with natural hesitation that I complied with Mr. Herman's request to write this short introduction. Of course, I played plenty of cricket when I had the time to swing a bat or bowl a ball. Actually my experience was moderately extensive, for I have known what it is like to be shot out by a speed merchant in Bermuda, and to be tricked by a spin expert in South Africa. I have even played in America, which is probably more than some of our Test stars can say. Of late the fine and great game has been clouded by controversies and quarrels. I suppose it is correct to say that persons like myself, with columns to fill, must bear a share of the responsibility; but I confess that big cricket, of the Test kind, has never appealed to me so much as the cricket which, for want of a better phrase, is known as the village green kind. In my youth I played much of that, and enjoyed it, but truthfully I cannot declare that I ever extracted the maximum of pleasure from watching a match between England and Australia. Nor did I ever find delight in composing the pieces that I realized would be widely read but that I also felt would help in saddling a fine pastime with a reputation it did not deserve. My first acquaintance with Mr. Herman was when he told me about a book he had made called Boxing for Beginners. That was a notable example of how such a volume should be written, but it seems to me that "How's That?" will chiefly supply a want that is as wide as a street. If cricket is to live it must catch the young, as the author asserts, when they are youthful enough to be taught. Very frequently it is stated that stars of the brightness of Donald Bradman never had a lesson. That I do not believe. Cricket cannot be picked up as the habit of smoking a cigarette may be contracted, and I know, to my sorrow, that if a book such as this had been on the market when I was tinkering with the scoring of runs I should not in my later years so often have been accused of perpetrating what were inelegantly described as cow shots. I am glad that Mr. Herman has gone out to capture the small boys and the slightly bigger boys.

It was a February night, and raining, and cold, when I first glanced over the manuscript of this book. It was no time for flannels, or for anything save a heated hearth and walls to keep out the whistles of the wind, but my spirit grew younger by the mere memories that were conjured up of faraway hours spent at mid-off, deep in the country, or at the crease.

Mr. Herman has again done well. But I warn him to be careful. At the rate he is proceeding he will shortly be known—and with good reason—as the Sporting Youngster's Counsellor and Friend. But he has this consolation. It is better to have this descriptive medal pinned on him now than to wait long enough for it to be used as an epitaph.

TREVOR WIGNALL.

THE TOSS

LET us get this right, from the start.

This does not pretend, in any way, to be an encyclopædia of Cricket.

It is a book for youngsters only—and, maybe, a few coaches.

I have tried to put in only what, I hope, will be useful to the growing generation.

I have a bee in my bonnet. And the bee that I hive is that we do not "catch 'em young enough." They do in Australia. Hence the present location of the "Ashes."

How many youngsters in Australia, or in South Africa, for that matter, would have to ask: "Where does Cover-Point stand?" Yet I have such questions asked me by members of good Preparatory School elevens.

I am hoping that this little book will be useful to chaps of about ten years to seventeen years of age. If it is I am amply repaid.

So, Good Luck to you all! I can wish you nothing better than a Good Game in Life—a long Innings, plenty of Wickets, and no missed Catches.

HOW'S THAT?

FIRST WICKET

BATTING: "POSITION" OR "STANCE"—WITH A WORD OR TWO ON KIT

STANCE

IT all depends on starting in the right way.

They say that "a good beginning makes a bad end." Well, that's true. A "good beginning" for the batsman makes a "bad end" for the bowler. It is quite impossible, though, to lay down hard-and-fast rules on how a batsman should stand while waiting for the ball to come, because, what may be a good starting position for one fellow may tie another in knots. Each person has his own peculiarities that way.

A great deal depends, of course, on your own make and build. A very tall chap may have to stoop a bit to get down to his bat. A little 'un will probably have to stand as upright as possible, to take full advantage of whatever height he has.

Some fellows can get a good sight of the ball by only turning their heads slightly to the left and looking sideways. Others can't see properly without facing the ball full with their eyes.

How to put your feet is a knotty point. One chap may feel awkward and unbalanced with his feet close together; while another is more easy, and can move more quickly from a similar position. Again, feet apart may be meat to one and cold poison to another. There are certain main principles to follow, all the same.

NOTE: If you are lucky enough to be a left-hander, you will have to reverse the positions given here. For instance, where it says "left foot" forward, that means "right foot" forward to you.

Let us start at the top.

HEAD

The HEAD should be turned, as much as is natural to you, towards the bowler. He wants watching—especially his hand and wrist. Tuck the chin into the left shoulder, something like a boxer. The left shoulder and elbow *must* point up the pitch.

As regards what direction you should face, you'll have to find that out for yourself—that is, how far you can turn your head and still get a good sight of the ball.

NOTE: You must be comfortable, and not feel stiff or awkward.

ALSO NOTE: Your head should be over your bat, so that head and bat are in the same line as the direction in which the ball is coming.

SHOULDER AND ELBOW

LEFT SHOULDER and LEFT ELBOW forward, sticking out towards the bowler.

"WAIT FOR IT"
NOTE.—Left shoulder well forward

NOTE: There is too much nowadays, especially in first-class cricket, of what is called the "Two-eyed Stance." That is—facing the bowler with the body square and shoulders in line. It is practically impossible, from this position, to cut or off-drive— two of the best scoring shots in cricket, and the most beautiful to watch. What more stirring sight is there than to watch F. E. Woolley cut a short ball so that it flashes past point like a swallow skimming the ground? Or to see that leopard-like leap of W. R. Hammond as he slams the over-pitched one past mid-off? Don't strokes like that thrill you? Don't you wish you could do the same? It all looks so easy. But it isn't. These chaps have only been able to do it after Practice and Practice to the *n*th degree. You *can* do it, too, on the same terms.

As a defensive position the "Two-eyed Stance" has its points. One can keep a ball, coming in from leg, out of the wicket more easily; but a batsman's job is, mainly, to score runs, not just to scratch about keeping his end up. There are a few chaps to whom this stance is natural, but not many. We had a case ourselves. A boy was making a fair number of runs in every match; but every time the bowler came up to bowl, he slewed himself round square. We tried hard at nets to get his left shoulder forward, with some success. His twenties and thirties became tens and fives, and, at last, a succession of blobs. So we let him have his own way. Back he went to his "Two-eyed Stance," and at once started making runs again. He was terribly awkward and clumsy, apparently—but effective. These cases are very few and far between.

No, there is no doubt whatever that the *Left Shoulder Stance* is by far the best in the vast majority of cases.

FEET

Now as to FEET. Footwork, as in boxing, is of the very greatest importance.

REMEMBER: It is your feet that get you where you want to be—that is, where the ball is. The weight should be on both feet with the legs bent slightly at the knees. Then you will feel "springy" and able to move into action quickly.

Whether you stand with feet together or apart is up to you. So long as you feel well balanced, and able to move in a hurry in any direction, it does not particularly matter. Legs *too* far apart, though, is "not a Good Thing." You see, if you start from the centre of a circle (your right foot being the centre or pivot), it is an easy matter to lunge out at a particular point on the circumference of that circle. If, on the other hand, your left foot is already out at the edge of the circle, and you suddenly find, owing to the ball breaking unexpectedly, that you have to shift it hurriedly to another point on that edge, you're going to find it jolly awkward to have to get there.

NOTE: Don't stand too far from your bat.

REMEMBER: Head and bat should be in line with the ball. If you're miles from your bat, it just can't be in that line.

Knees

Note: Do not bend the knees too much. It will make you awkward, and waste time straightening up. Some people like to have the feet apart—others together. Find out for yourself in what position you feel most comfortable, but—

Remember: You must be able to move quickly.

Note: If your right foot is parallel with the crease, and the left foot at an angle of at least 45 degrees to it, pointing towards the bowler, you will not go far wrong. Besides, your left knee and foot won't get in the light, if you have to bring your bat down somewhat rapidly in order to keep a "Yorker" out of your wicket.

Guard

Note: When taking guard, make sure that the block and your right foot are well within the crease. Wicket-keepers nowadays are pretty smart. There is a note on the different guards at the end of the "Second Wicket."

Handle Grip

Do not grip the handle of the bat too far down. You will have no control over it if you do. Suppose you held a tennis-racket or golf-club down at the end of the handle—look pretty funny, wouldn't you? About half-way up the handle is best.

Note: The hands should be nearly, or actually, touching. Too far apart is a mistake. Once more

"FORWARD DEFENCE"
NOTE.—The ball was slightly short and popping up

it is a question of control. If the hands are near together, they have a better chance of working together. If they are far away from each other, they are apt to work independently. Your right hand may want to cut, while the left chooses to drive, then up trots the umpire to replace the bails. The left hand has the main grip. The right is a sort of direction controller. In a few leg strokes, however, the right sometimes takes charge.

Eyes

REMEMBER: Keep your eyes glued on the bowler's hand and wrist. When the ball leaves his hand, transfer your rapt gaze to that ball—and keep it there until a kindly spectator returns it from the boundary. Always try to move so that your eyes are directly in the line of flight of the ball.

Kit

A word about Kit. Without being a tailor's dummy, see to it that your clothes are clean and fairly loose fitting. Too tight clothes are a nuisance and may spoil your batting by taking your attention from the job in hand.

BOOTS are very important. Never have any spikes missing if you can help it. Just one little slip on a damp wicket, and you hear the horrible rattle of the batsman's "Last Post" behind you. Then you will want to choose a quiet spot behind the pavilion and gently kick yourself for not having had those spikes put in. It is wise to wear—

BATTING GLOVES: There are two main kinds—the "draw-on" and the kind that "winds" up round the wrist. Choose whichever gives you the best grip on that bat handle.

NOTE: PADS. *Always* wear *both* pads. Do not have them too tight. A bit too big is better than a bit too small, both for reasons of economy—if you are still growing, you will grow into them—and because, with the exertion of running about, your legs swell a little. Strap them up with the buckles outside.

BAT

Last, but hardly least, the BAT. *Please, please, please—*

REMEMBER: Never use a bat too large for you. It cramps your style. It is hard to control, oh! and a thousand and one other reasons too numerous to put down. The top of the blade should be about in line with your knee. The tragedies we have witnessed through boys using their fathers' bats! Why, even Don Bradman's two hundreds would have been twenties if he had used a barn-door bat when young.

When choosing your bat, be very careful that it suits you. Better too light than too heavy. Play imaginary strokes with it—especially trying the back-swing. If it seems to come up without much effort on your part, then that is the best bat for you. Look at the seams. They should be straight and not too narrow. About seven is the best number of seams. See that there are no knot-holes.

NOTE: Finally, always have a rubber handle grip.

Now that we have kept the bowler standing like a statue on the crease for long enough, let us let him go.

SECOND WICKET

"Still Batting"—"The Strokes"

Ready Position

As the bowler's arm comes round, get ready. The ready position is like this: Raise the left heel slightly so as to "Be Prepared," as the Scouts say, to move in a hurry, but keep the right foot flat. You will see why later. Bend the left elbow and lift the bat behind you, so that left elbow, wrist and bat form more or less a straight line.

Note: Do not move the head.

Note: Always try to get into such a position that your head is well over the ball when the bat hits it—the ball, not your head! Eye, bat, ball and bowler's hand should be in *one straight line*.

Resist, with all the power you've got, the temptation to let your eye wander from any view, however attractive, than that of the bowler's hand. This is terribly important. Even the fascinating vision of your own spotless boots, beautiful pads, or latest-thing-in-batting gloves, must not be allowed to twist your gaze from the job of work in hand, i.e., watching the bowler, his hand in particular. Few bowlers can really disguise what they mean to do. A telltale flick of the wrist usually gives the game away. And if you don't see that flick, then you won't know what to expect. And that will be, so to speak, just that. Anyway, you'll regret it on your lone, lorn, long trudge back to the pavilion, amid a chilly silence, as the scorer calls to the score-board operator: "251 for 2, last man BLOB!"

PITCH OF BALL

All now depends on where the ball pitches. That is why you must watch it like a hawk. If it pitches on a spot that you can reach with your bat, come right out at it, and chuck your left foot towards it, at the same time pointing that left foot towards the bowler. Also, at the same time bring down the bat to it, but—REMEMBER: Keep the left shoulder and elbow well forward. When the bat hits the ball, your head should be well over the hitting spot. Also the handle of the bat should be pushed well forward. That is to keep the ball well down "on the carpet." If the bat is slanting away from you, or even straight up, the ball is bound to rise.

Have you ever played billiards? Right. What happens when you hit the cushion at an angle? Does the ball come down and back to you? "No, no, a thousand times no!" It goes on and *up* the table. So will a cricket-ball if your bat is even straight up. "How much more, then," as the geom. books say, will it rise if the end of your bat is slanting forward?

NOTE: THE RIGHT FOOT HAS NOT MOVED. Now you know why you keep it flat. If you are as quick on your feet as a streak of lightning, as Charlie Macartney used to be, you can dance down the wicket to get the pitch of the ball, but, until you

"AS THE BOWLER'S ARM COMES ROUND"
Note.—He is ready for practically any stroke

have reached that point of perfection, *please* keep that right foot *still*.

I've heard an old cricket coach threaten a lad, whose right foot was apt to wander: "Ah'll peg that theer fooot daown, sirr, that Ah will." He never actually carried the threat into operation. But it makes one feel like wanting to do it, when a batsman's right foot starts edging coyly in the direction of the square-leg umpire. Besides, you depend on your right foot as a pivot, and, if that pivot shifts, you have no centre to work from. So how can you possibly regulate the direction in which you should really go?

Now, suppose you are pretty sure that you cannot reach out to where the ball pitches, then play back. That is, keep the left foot still and step back towards the wicket with the right foot.

REMEMBER two things, though. (a) Do not step too far back and make a mess of your wicket, and (b) do not step in front of your wicket unless the ball is well on the off and not breaking in. Bring the bat down straight, but still keep the left arm forward so that the bat is at such an angle that the ball returns to Mother Earth.

NOTE: You can step with your right foot back in front of your wicket for a leg stroke—*if* the ball is off the wicket. This is for two reasons: (a) you can't be l.b.w. (b) you can get more power into a sweep to leg, and knock holes through square-leg.

REMEMBER: Except for a hook or a cut THE STRAIGHT BAT RULES THE WORLD. Keep that bat utterly perpendicular.

TRY THIS: For about ten minutes every evening of your life, stand in front of a mirror—the taller the better. Put a piece of tape on the floor leading towards the middle of the mirror. Take a bat and stand with your toes about three inches clear of the tape, and take up the starting position. In slow motion get back to the ready position, then—all in slow motion, mind—play a forward stroke along the white line.

NOTE: Watch in the mirror that the bat is dead straight all the way. Finish the stroke without a follow through. Your left foot should finish up parallel to the tape. (If your right foot has moved, stamp on it, and put it back to where it started!) The bottom of the bat should be on the tape about half-way along your left foot. The handle will be well canted forward, with, as usual, left shoulder, elbow and wrist well forward. When you find it becomes too easy in slow motion, quicken up gradually until you find you can do it at a decent pace without making mistakes. By the way, do not get too near the mirror—for obvious reasons. You want to make a run or two in the next seven years!

You can also practise this at odd moments on the field along a crease. In that case, though, you will not have the advantage of seeing your mistakes glaring at you from a mirror.

NOTE: All the strokes so far have been defensive. You have not let the bat follow through so that it would really smite the ball and make it disappear to the middle distance. The ball has merely hit the bat, so to speak. Now let us pretend to cane that ball. Back to the old mirror again.

REMEMBER: Always start in slow motion.

Now, instead of stopping the bat by your foot, let it follow right through, so that it ends up by pointing in the air. *But* please do not swing either to the right-hand or to the left. It must finish still in line with the tape. Of course not every ball comes straight for the stumps. There are such things as off- and leg-balls. When you are certain you have got the straightforward shot, try changing direction a bit. It is not a bad scheme to choose an unused patch of ground, make a block-hole and mark out a half a dozen lines leading from it—four to the off and two a little to leg in about the direction of mid-on. Do not make too much mess, though. Now practise your forward strokes along these lines. In winter you can obtain some more tape and do it at home.

By the way, when you have finished, do pack up that tape neatly, and tidy up. Don't leave it about for someone else to clear up, because it wouldn't be sporting, you know. A *real* cricketer is *never* selfish.

REMEMBER: Do not try the follow-through until you are sure you can play the ordinary forward stroke. In all these strokes—NOTE that the left hand does the main work and the right hand is merely a guide.

When the time of the lawn-mower comes, and that most enchanting of all smells, new-cut grass, get as much open-air practice as you can.

Doesn't that grassy smell seem to draw you?

Don't visions rise up of a "sound for a smite for six," the rattle of a batsman's "timber-yard" when you've got him where you want him, or the "smack" of a well-judged catch?

TRY THIS: Get a friend to stand about seven yards in front of you with a ball. Take your bat and let him lob the ball up at you straight. You can now put into practice all the strokes you have been trying in theory. Have mercy on him, though, and let him have his whack too! It's all very well "trying it on the dog." The dog wants his "day" too, you know!

Later on we will see what to do about net practice.

Now we know a bit about playing forward let us try playing back to the short ball. This is a defensive stroke, except for cuts and glides. Though people like W. R. Hammond can force a ball to the boundary while playing back, with you that will come in time. Still, always play back hard and firmly. A floppy back stroke is dangerous, as it may make the bat turn in your hand. Then the slips will leap for it with joy, or a still small "How's That?" will come from the wicket-keeper. Besides, cricket and floppiness or sloppiness don't go particularly well together, do they? One always likes to think of a cricketer as a firm, reliable sort of chap.

NOTE: In a defensive back stroke, turn so that you face the bowler squarely. Still keep that bat straight. Try the old mirror stunt; it will help.

TRY THIS: Get your long-suffering friend to stand with a bat in front of the wicket. Stand yourself about five yards up the pitch. If your pal plays an imaginary back stroke with the bat at an angle, NOTE how much of the wicket is covered. See the difference?

The shorter a ball is pitched, the higher you will have to lift your bat, naturally. If a ball is pitched so short that it becomes a long hop, one can sometimes play half-forward to it and crack it hard. A long hop to the off you can drive hard, or cut. To leg you can pull it round past Square-leg. But be careful if it is on the wicket.

A rank, bad long hop has often taken a wicket, because the batsman was inclined to be careless. G. T. S. Stevens, of Middlesex, once bowled W. H. Ponsford, of Australia, in a Test Match at the Oval, with the longest of long hops ever seen! It pitched about ten yards short of the wicket, reared up, and just dropped on to the wicket with a happy little sigh! Ponsford made a perfectly wild shot at it.

The chief scoring strokes in back play are the Cut and the Glide.

REMEMBER: Only use these strokes on shortish balls off the wicket. Play a straight-bat-back-stroke to anything on the wicket. If you are not sure if it is a straight ball or not, pretend that it is a straight ball, and *do not* try to cut or glide.

THE CUT

The cut is, perhaps, the hardest stroke of all to play perfectly, and needs a terrible lot of practice. There are three kinds of cut—the square cut, the ordinary cut, the late cut.

"JUST WHAT THE BOWLER WANTED"
NOTE.—He's nibbled and edged a very off ball

The Square Cut

The square cut travels approximately in the direction of point, and should only be used on a very short and fairly wide ball. When you have made up your mind to square cut, throw the left leg across—the wider the ball, the farther that leg must go. Bring the bat downwards towards the ball, so that, at the moment of hitting, the bat is almost horizontal. Do it with some vigour, though.

NOTE: The fact of the blade of the bat should be slanting so that the ball is forced down, not up. That is the great difficulty about the stroke, of course—keeping the ball down. Let your left wrist do the work, and you will find it comes quite easily.

NOTE: Stick the left shoulder and elbow well out towards Cover. That'll make the ball fairly whizz along its appointed journey to its destination on the distant boundary.

The Ordinary Cut

The ordinary cut goes in the direction of about third man. In this stroke throw the right foot out towards third man, but—NOTE: Do not shift the left foot. Now bring the bat round, and down, as in a square cut, but not so far, because this is not a forcing stroke. In this case the ball hits the bat, sort of runs along the blade of the bat, and shoots off—we hope—to the boundary. Try and dodge third man

HOBBS CUTTING
Just perfect

Keystone View Company

[Sport & General

"ENDEAVOUR"
Maurice Tate literally "in action"

by holding the point of the bat a little to left or right of him, as the case may be.

AGAIN NOTE: Take care that the blade of your bat is sloping at an angle of about 45 degrees to the pitch. Then the ball won't rise, but shoot down to the ground, which is where you want it.

THE LATE CUT

Now for the late cut.

The idea of this shot is to dodge the wicket-keeper and first slip, or to send the ball flashing between the slips. But do not try off too short a ball. DON BRADMAN has such remarkable eyesight that he can late cut a ball within an inch or two of the off stump. Don't you try that yet, though. Maybe later! This stroke gives the wicket-keeper little chance if he is standing up to the wicket. It is played with a straight bat. Once more, let the ball hit the bat with the face of the blade of the bat turned towards cover point. Push the handle of the bat outwards, though, so that the ball will not pop up into the slips' ever-waiting hands. This really means that you are just turning the ball from its course.

REMEMBER in this, as well as in most strokes, try to get into such a position that your head is well over the point of contact between bat and ball.

TRY THIS: Get your pal again to stand half-way up the pitch, in a net, and bring them down to you short, or shortish, so that you can practise all these cuts.

The Leg Glide

The leg glide is a sort of late cut reversed.

NOTE: Once again the ball hits the bat and is deflected off its course. RANJITSINHJI reduced leg gliding to an exact science, and was even known, on occasions, to lift his left foot and leg-glide between his legs, and, once or twice, between the bat and his pads, thus unsighting the leg-side fieldsmen.

Square-Leg Hit or Sweep

If a ball is too short to glide, and well wide of the wicket, throw your left leg towards it, swing your bat square down and round on it, and let it go so that Square-leg will wish he was not there.

NOTE: The ball must be forced down towards the ground, so keep the face of the bat slightly facing the ground. Perhaps your pal will sacrifice himself again, and heave a few short ones down at you on the leg side.

When you are practising all these shots, stick, and stick, and stick at it till you can do them well. Then go on practising them, or the polish will wear off, and you will get rusty.

A few words about special types of balls.

Yorker

A YORKER is a ball that pitches straight and on or about the crease. It is a beast. You cannot

"GOT IT!"
NOTE.—The Square-Leg Umpire had to jump for his life

score from it, so just bring a straight bat down on top of it, hitting ball and ground at the same time. Left elbow forward, though, or it will pop up.

Full Pitch

A Full Pitch comes to you without hitting the ground. If it is off the wicket, and not too high, you are safe in having a crack at it. But if it is on the wicket, "have a care and be exceeding careful." Just play back with a straight bat, and be content to keep it off your wicket. A straight full pitch is a treacherous business. Even Jack Hobbs was tempted by one from Arthur Mailey in a Test match at the Oval—it got him, middle peg!

Remember: Never hit across the break. That takes a bit of explaining.

Off-Break

An Off-Break comes in towards you from the off. Hit along the line of the break to the off. Do not try to pull it to leg. The same with a Leg-Break.

Note though—if a ball is pitched so dreadfully short, and comes in from the off, so that you have plenty of time to judge it well, by all means have a go at whanging it round to leg. Take care it is not on the wicket, though, as you may regret it.

A Leg-Break should go to leg. If you hit across the break, there is only one wee fraction of a second, while the bat is crossing the line of the ball, in which your bat can possibly connect with it. Whereas, if you hit along the line of the break, your bat is in the direct path of the ball, and is much more likely to hit it. The same applies to a swerving ball. Allow for the swerve and hit along the line at which the ball comes at you.

NOTE: A ball pitched on the wicket and going away to leg should give the square-leg umpire "gip." Also a ball going away to the off, if wide enough, should drill a hole through Point.

NOTE: A ball too near the wicket to cut should be left severely alone.

If your eye is very, very good, you may risk trying to cut a short-leg break that pitches on the wicket and goes away. This stroke will need a terrible lot of practice, though.

And please *never, never* pull an off-ball round to leg. It may come off once in fifty times. But most of the other forty-nine times it will mean disaster.

REMEMBER: Watch the ball like a hawk *always*. Try to see it right up to the moment your bat connects with it.

NOTE: You can always play forward more on a hard dry pitch. A sticky wicket holds the ball back more.

RUNNING

A word about the sadly neglected, but most important, art of running.

NOTE: Get into the habit of calling "Yes," or "No," or "Wait" for every ball. And don't be afraid to call out good and loud. Nothing is so apt to confuse your partner and give the fieldsmen confidence as a timid, little, rabbit-like whisper. Do not dither. Make up your mind at once, and stick to it. It is awful to see a batsman hesitating, going backwards and forwards, and generally pottering about. Don't be a "Yes—no"-er!

If you are at the batting end, run well clear of the pitch on the same side the bowler is bowling. If you are at the other end, back up as the bowler bowls, and run well clear of the pitch.

It is not well to back up before the ball has left the bowler's hand. Don't forget that the ball is "in play" as soon as the bowler starts his run; and, if you are out of your crease, he can put down the wicket and run you out. It is an unwritten law of cricket sportsmanship, though, that the first time he offends he is warned by the bowler. The next time he will definitely be "for it."

REMEMBER: You should never cross the pitch. This is so that the pitch will not be damaged, and thus help the bowler. That wily gentleman will always take advantage of any patch that may be caused by your spikes. And rightly, too, because it will be your own fault.

Always run the first run *hard*, then look round for a chance of another.

NOTE: When you are about two or three yards from the other end, slide your bat, edge down, along the ground, in front of you, until it is just over the crease, then turn round, and be prepared for another run. This saves time. The rules tell you that you are "in" if either the bat or some part of your person is over the crease. On the crease counts definitely as "out." Also the run will not count if your bat is not over the crease. The umpire will quickly yell "One Short."

This "over the crease" business counts in being stumped, too. So watch the right foot, and keep it still.

Finally, about taking guard—or centre. Everybody has his own ideas about what suits him in this matter.

NOTE: Keep the right foot well inside the crease. If you have the habit of standing very near your bat, take "middle and leg." Otherwise "centre" is usually the best. Though, against a leg-break bowler, it is sometimes as well to take middle and leg.

Guards

```
x  x  x
   —       Centre or Middle Stump.
x  x  x
   —       Middle and Off (very rare).
x  x  x
      —    Middle and Leg or "covering two"
x  x  x
      —    Leg Stump or "covering one."
x  x  x
—          Off Stump (very rarely taken).
```

So to the opposite end of the pitch, and let us see what the bowler's plan of campaign is.

THIRD WICKET

"Bowling"

Golden Rules

Perhaps your ambition is to be a bowler.

Bowling has its thrills in plenty. It is a great feeling to be able to test a batsman, and find out what sort of ball he does not like, and suddenly to let him have it. Really, when you come to think of it, bowling is the most important thing in the game. It's the brainiest part of cricket. The bowler has the initiative. *He* works out his scheme. After all, the batsman has to play according to what sort of ball the bowler chooses to send down.

First of all, get your run up to the wicket. That is to say, find out what length of run suits you best. The faster you bowl, the longer your run should be. This rule doesn't always hold. I knew a fast bowler once who only took three short steps and then plugged down an in-swinger from leg. He was very tall—about six feet six inches long!—with exceptionally long arms, and left-handed. His run was curious, too. He had the umpire as near the wicket as possible. (Note: The umpire has to stand where the bowler wants him, always provided that he has a clear view down the pitch.) Then he started with his back towards the batsman, swung his body suddenly round the umpire, round the wicket, and made full use of his height. Still, he was a freak. He took stacks of wickets in Country House Cricket. He was also the Squire's chauffeur!

NOTE: Avoid too long a run. It only tires you out.

You are allowed one foot over the bowling crease. In the case of a right-hander it will be the left foot; for a left-hander the right foot. But—

REMEMBER: If the back foot so much as touches the crease, the umpire will lift his hand in horror, and yell "No Ball." Also—

NOTE: The bowling arm must not be bent, when the ball is delivered, otherwise it counts as a throw, which counts as a "No Ball."

The history of over-arm bowling is rather interesting. Until about 1820 no bowler was allowed to bowl over-arm. That is, he had to bowl "lobs," with the hand below the elbow. After that date, and a lot of argument, round-arm bowling was allowed. Though still with the hand below the shoulder. In 1822 a certain John Willes found that by bowling with his arm well up, over the shoulder, he could make the ball do all sorts of funny things. So he tried it in a Kent *v.* M.C.C. match at Lord's. But the umpire was horrified and no-balled him umpteen times. Master Willes immediately mounted his horse and rode away in disgust! The cricket field knew him no more. But the effect remained, and, a few years later, in 1835, the M.C.C. altered the rules so that over-arm bowling was legal. But the arm has to be kept straight, and not bent at the elbow. Nor must the ball be jerked.

When you are satisfied that you can run up to the crease, get your front foot over it, and your back foot well behind it at the moment of bowling, without having to watch the crease the whole time, then measure the length of the run in paces. Stick to that run always, in matches, games or nets. Go on practising this run until it comes natural to you.

NOTE: Always make a little mark, just big enough to see, on the ground, where your run begins. Soon you will get so used to this run up that you will be able to do what every bowler should do for every ball he bowls. That is—to keep your eye on the wicket at which you are bowling, right from the beginning of your run.

Now comes the great question—are you going to bowl round the wicket or over it? Round the wicket means that your bowling arm will be outside, away from the bowler's wicket, and your back will be towards the umpire. This is usually reserved for slow bowlers. Over, or across the wicket, means that the bowling arm will be between your body and the wicket. Most bowlers bowl over the wicket, especially medium and fast bowlers. Some bowlers, who bowl across as a rule, like to bowl round to a left-handed batsman. That is up to you. If you feel like it, do it. You may find that, by bowling round the wicket to a left-hander, you get a better sight of the wicket.

Try bowling across first. If you have a sort of idea that you can bowl better round, by all means try it. *But*—if you find that it does not make you bowl any better, drop it.

The disadvantage of bowling round the wicket is that you only get a sight of the batsman's wicket at the last moment, as you are unsighted by the umpire. Most round-the-wicket bowlers have to mike from behind that obstructive umpire.

Hold on! Here it is! The Main Point! A bowler *must* have *length, length, length.* That is to say, he must be able to pitch the ball pretty well where he likes. A bowler without a *length* is like a fish without a backbone. In fact, he is a mere jellyfish—and about as much use.

People talk glibly about So-and-so being able to "pitch a ball on a sixpence." Oh, can he? Let me assure you that no bowler who ever lived could, with any certainty, pitch near an envelope, much less a sixpence. Even Wilfred Rhodes, S. F. Barnes, Hedley Verity and Grimmett—four of the most accurate bowlers of modern times—would laugh at the very idea. But there is no harm in trying to be as accurate as possible, is there?

TRY THIS: Peg down a double sheet of newspaper, end on, about two yards in front of the batsman's crease. Now bowl one over, and see how many balls you can pitch *on* that paper. Not so jolly easy, is it? This newspaper idea is rather good. Try it every day for a few overs. When you have become fairly accurate and can hit the paper most times, fold it over, and try the single sheet. Now you can try shifting it backwards and forwards a foot or two. Because—

NOTE: A good-length ball is a ball that pitches about a foot and a half *in front* of where a batsman can reach when playing right forward. This gets him in two minds. He is not sure if he can reach it or not. If he plays forward, he is apt to put the ball up, and you will get him caught. If he plays back, he may be too late, and you will make a mess of his wicket. So, obviously, you will have to bowl rather shorter to a tall chap than to a little 'un. But do not be afraid of pitching it up to the batsman, though. A long hop is easy meat to batsmen.

This is worth repeating—in fact, it should be written up somewhere in letters of fire: REMEMBER, LENGTH IS EVERYTHING. So practise it, and practise it. And when you have done that, then go on practising it.

As you have seen by now, accuracy is absolutely necessary to a bowler. *Never* be satisfied with yourself. Even though you have done pretty well, *remember*—you can always do better. So go on trying to improve yourself. TRY THIS: Shove the old paper down and bowl at one stump only. Go on doing this until you can pitch on it, and hit the stumps a few times.

REMEMBER: It doesn't matter two hoots how long it takes you to hit that stump. It is worth going on trying, and trying, and trying. It is a grand feeling to be able to drop a ball pretty well where you want it to go. Besides, all your "best-laid schemes" will "gang agley," if you can't; and it's the batsman who will have the laugh over you.

Fancy unleashing that pet off-break of yours, only to find that you have dropped it too short, and that demon batsman has carted it over the leg boundary.

F. R. Spofforth, who was probably the greatest bowler who ever lived, used to bowl a few imaginary overs every day. Even in his office in the winter he used to swing his arm round, and pretend that he was bowling in a Test Match for Australia against England. He always said that this practice helped Australia to beat England more than once.

A slow bowler should be easy to play—in theory. Obviously, when the ball is coming slowly, the batsman has heaps of time in which to make up his mind what he is going to do with it. Yet, for season after season, little Freeman, of Kent, the slowest bowler in first-class Cricket, headed the averages, usually taking over two hundred wickets. Lots of times a slow bowler has started a rot, and put the wind up the other side. You have probably seen it happen yourself.

By the way, it's a curious business—this "starting a rot." And it so often happens. The first pair of batsmen are well set. The wicket is easy and the bowling not too bad. A new bowler, a slow merchant, is put on. He takes a short run and sends down a slow long hop. With a grateful heart, and a thrill of anticipation, the batsman gathers himself together and has a go. He has visions, poor chap, of broken glass in the pavilion, the umpire signalling a "six," and distant cheering on the boundary. But the unexpectedness of it all has slightly affected his judgment. There is an almost inaudible click—and first slip accepts the gift gladly. The following batsman, telling himself to be careful, plays back to the next half-volley. There is a deadly silence as the umpire replaces the bails. That settles it! Batsman after batsman creeps coyly behind his bat. The field draws closer and closer in. Nice little dolly catches pop up into large, red, eager, waiting hands. Unless the side can boast a man of considerably more than average determination, then the whole tragedy is complete.

This has happened in all types of cricket—even in Test Matches. School matches, though, are most affected by this sort of thing, because so much depends on the result, and so many critical, or hopeful, eyes are watching that batsmen are not quite themselves. They suspect deep-laid pitfalls and traps that, probably, do not exist.

The cure, of course, is for one man to go in and play his natural game. Just one decent crack past cover, and the flock of vultures, waiting for that dolly catch, will retire thoughtfully to the middle distance. The slow bowler will now find his long hops and half-volleys treated at their face value. Soon he will have to retreat to deep third man and chew grass. For another will have taken his place at the crease.

But the "rot" will have stopped!

Why should a good slow bowler be difficult to play? Well, the slower you bowl, the more control you have over the ball. So the slow fellow can make the ball "do" more. Leg-breaks, off-breaks, googlies—that is off-breaks with a leg-break action, or vice versa—can all be used to make a batsman gnash his teeth. A damp or drying wicket which

"JUST COMING OVER"
NOTE.—Left arm helping swing

grips the ball a bit, and so adds to the effect of the spin, is the slow bowler's paradise. This is the way it happens. After the rain has done its worst, and the turf is well soaked, out comes the sun and bakes the surface, making a hard upper crust. The ball pitches on that crust, and makes a slight dent. If the ball is coming slowly enough, the sides of the dent will have time to take the spin, and change the direction of the ball. The same thing happens when a billiards table cushion takes the spin of a billiards ball.

But, oh! *remember* none of these things is of the slightest use if the ball is not of *good length*. If you pitch too short, the batsman has any amount of time to spot the direction of the break, and can act accordingly. If you over-pitch, he has time to get it before it breaks, either full pitch or half-volley.

We will have a word or two to say about how to make a ball break later.

If your natural pace is medium, you will have to cultivate a few tricks. You will not be fast enough to get wickets by sheer pace, nor slow enough to make the ball do much. You can do a lot, though, by little variations of length. If you have a good command of length, a ball dropping just a shade shorter, after several well pitched up, will often catch a batsman napping. He will not expect it, and he has not so much time in which to think. Later on, after any amount of practice, you can start trying to make the ball turn a bit. You cannot get on such a big break as a slow bowler can, of course, but you may be able to make it change direction enough to beat the bat.   More on this subject later.

Then again, you may be able to swerve the ball, that is, to make it swing in the air, before it pitches, from leg or off.   This is a little overdone nowadays, and most batsmen are wise to it.   Still, if bowling into the wind, or with a cross wind, it may be useful. In the next "Wicket" we will see how it is done.

Now for the fast bowler.   Good fast bowlers are needed badly these days.   Years ago no team would have thought of taking the field without, at least, one really fast bowler.   Two for choice.

I played against a team of Sikhs in India.   They had five good and fast bowlers in their team!   That's overdoing it, though.   The novelty wears off, and the batsman gets the "contempt bred by familiarity."   In other words he gets so used to it that it becomes easy to deal with.

But—please do not try it too soon.   Make sure that you are a natural fast bowler before you take it up.   If, when you try to bowl fast, you are not sure in which direction the ball is going, or where it is going to pitch, then cut fast bowling out of your programme.   Many a jolly good slow, or medium, bowler has been spoilt by trying to bowl too fast. His length goes all to rags.   And that is the end of him as a bowler.

Also, if you find that bowling fast takes *too* much effort, then it is not natural to you.   You are merely straining yourself.

NOTE: Just pure pace, and nothing else, is hopeless.   You may frighten one or two rabbits; but that is not Cricket.   A fast bowler needs length as much as any other kind of bowler. The advantage he has is that the batsman has less time in which to shape for his stroke. He certainly has no time to change his mind.

The fast bowler who can make the ball "talk" a bit is a very rare bird indeed. Maybe, after lots of practice, you will have such a fine command of length that you will be able to do it, without losing that length. When that time comes, you will be welcomed in any team. There is a bit more coming about this.

Finally, the bowler who "mixes 'em up." The bowler who can change his pace is very useful. The batsman gets panicky, because he does not know what is coming next.

Maurice Tate, of England and Sussex, can change his pace beautifully, without altering his action at all. He often had the Australians tied up completely, because they could not tell, from the loose swing of those immense shoulders, whether that extra pacy one was coming, or whether that innocent-looking little demon of the slow spinner was on its way.

NOTE: It must be done without altering your action at all, though, which is not easy. The whole effect will be spoilt if you give the game away by suddenly changing your run, charging up to the wicket, and slinging in a speedy one. You might just as well send a wire: "Fast 'un coming love Horace." And, of course, it is useless to change pace if your length goes to pieces. Do not try the variety act if you are not perfectly sure of your length. Please do not get bored with this word *length*. It is as important to a bowler as wheels are to a car.

A last tip.

REMEMBER: Always stick to your wicket. As soon as a ball is hit, get behind your wicket, like a wicket-keeper, as soon as you can.

NOTE: Do not stand between the ball and the wicket. It only wastes time. Besides, an accurate throw from a fieldsman might have hit the wicket, if you had not been in the light. Always go for any possible catch, of course. But do not baulk your fieldsman. If anything is going to Mid-off or Mid-on, let 'em have it. Trust your field. Even if, as sometimes happens, they let you down, grin and bear it, and go on trying.

Now we will have a shot at the finer points of bowling.

FOURTH WICKET

Bowling: On Again

Now that we know how to control the ball, we can go a step or two further.

A slow bowler has to be up to all sorts of tricks.

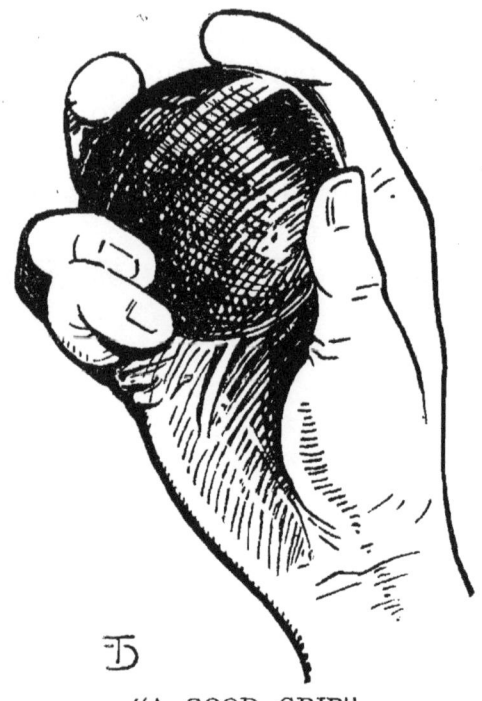

"A GOOD GRIP"
Note.—She's going to turn from the off

Chief among them is a break. To break a ball, you have to get so much spin on it that, when it pitches, it will change direction sharply. There are two main breaks—the off-break, which comes into the batsman from the off, or in front of him, and the leg-break, which turns in to him from the leg side.

To bowl an *Off-Break*, hold the ball firmly between the thumb and the first two fingers. The seam should be slanting from the top right to bottom left, that is from north-east to south-west. As you deliver the ball, give the thumb and fingers a twist to the right, and turn the wrist in the same way at the same time. The ball will then be spinning clock-wise. When the ball hits the ground, it will "change direction right," as they say in the Army

NOTE: You will have to pitch an off-break on or outside the off peg. But, if you have some good fieldsman to leg, you may get the batsman caught by pitching straight or to leg. Do not overdo this, though, as a fellow with a long reach and a good eye may easily cart it over the square-leg boundary, especially if you bowl at all short. The off-break is the easiest and most natural break. This is because it is easier to turn the hands inwards than outwards.

On the other hand, most batsmen, if they are right-handed, find an off-break easier to deal with than the leg species. You see, the ball comes in towards the batsman from in front, and he has no need to twist himself round to face it.

To the left-hander, of course, the off-break becomes a leg-break, and is more difficult to play. It's curious how many left-handers are good at playing the leg-break, though. I suppose, knowing the disadvantage they are at in having to play what is, to them, a difficult ball, and which most bowlers find it easy to bowl, they practise dealing with the said nuisance as much as possible. So, after a time, it becomes quite easy to them.

Philip Mead, Hampshire and England, was particularly strong on the leg, even for a left-hander. I saw Mead do a most amusing thing at the Oval once. He was sometimes rather dreary to watch. He had a cast-iron defence, and endless patience. So, if the bowling was good, he just waited till the inevitable loose one came along, and smacked it hard. The crowd towards square-leg (the recognized "barrack square" at the Oval) grew restive as Mead plodded on at the rate of about 17 runs an hour. Groans and cat-calls were followed by ironical cheering every time a single was scored. Suddenly, with a broad smile, the humorist Mead let go, and hit a terrific six to leg, scattering the gay barrackers in all directions.

The *Leg-Break* is not so easy. Instead of that twist to the right, you have to give the ball a turn to the left—which does not seem so natural. If you have the luck to be a left-hander, the leg-break is simple to you. It is what the off-break is to the common or garden right-hander.

Now for how to do it—hold the ball with the thumb below and the first three fingers on top, taking care to tuck the little finger modestly away as far as it will go by curling it up. It is the sleeping partner in this concern. As the ball leaves your hand, give your wrist a turn outwards, flick the thumb upwards, and straighten out the little finger.

The back of the hand should be towards you as

the ball leaves it. Sounds rather complicated, all this, doesn't it? Still, I told you it is hard to do.

Some chaps bowl leg-breaks naturally. It just seems to come without effort. If you are one of that lucky band, check up on the above explanation, and see if it fits.

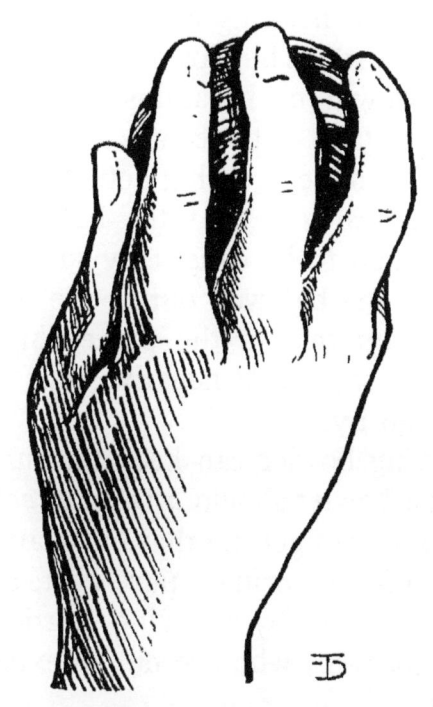

"JUST BEFORE A LEG-BREAK"
NOTE.—The wrist will have to bend right over

Just a word or two more on this leg-break business.

NOTE: The ball should be held with the seam slanting from north-west to south-east.

REMEMBER: This is the most difficult break to bowl, still keeping a length. So it wants any amount of practice. We will reserve the googly until later.

By the way, the googly is called a bosie in Australia, because B. J. T. Bosanquet was the first to tie up the Aussies with it. Clarence Grimmett has now well out-bosied Bosie!

One approaches the question of swerve very carefully. It is rather overdone nowadays.

Swerves which swing away from the wicket are the commonest. They are bowled in the hope that the batsman will mis-hit and get the ball on the edge of the bat instead of the centre, thus giving the slips or fine-leg a chance. What actually happens in the majority of cases is that the batsman, not being chump enough to be caught by such a rabbit-trap, merely lifts his bat well out of the light and takes no further interest in the proceedings. I always think of this somewhat negative stuff as "Watching the trains go by!"

A swerving bowler can keep the runs down, it is true. But a bowler should *attack, attack* and *attack*, with the object of getting that batsman out. Merely to stop him from scoring is pure waste of time. Still, wickets can be got by swerving, particularly among the later goers-in, who are not so experienced. So here goes.

You can make the ball turn in the air before it pitches either from the off or the leg. If there is a wind blowing straight up the pitch towards you, it can help a lot. A cross wind blowing towards you is very useful, too.

To swerve a ball from the off, hold it with the first and second fingers over the top, pointing towards the unfortunate batsman. The seam should be on a slant, so that the top side runs along under the second finger. For the swerve from leg, hold the ball in the same way, except that the first finger should lie along the seam. In both cases, you must get your arm as high as possible at the moment of delivery, and let your arm follow through well. This is called "making the ball go with your arm."

A left-arm bowler is always an awkward fellow to deal with—if he has a good length, of course. You see, a ball coming in from leg on to the wicket is one of the most difficult for a batsman to play. This is partly because he has to waste time turning round to it, and partly because he has to readjust his line of vision by turning his head. And a left-hander's natural break is from leg. So, if you are a left-hander, and can bowl a bit, it will be worth your while to practise that length.

A good left-arm bowler is well worth his salt on any side. Think of poor Colin Blythe, a true artist, who was killed in the Great War, Frank Woolley, in his bowling days, W. Rhodes, Voce, many others too numerous to mention, and now Fleetwood-Smith of Australia. Any one of these was, or is, capable of changing the whole aspect of a match in half an hour.

Now for a few general tips.

NOTE: A bowler should always work to his field.

Put all your trust in the efficiency of the fieldsmen. Even if a soft catch is put down on the "carpet," just grin, and say: "Hard luck, old chap. You'll get it next time." That is team work—without which a bowler is lost.

E

Glance round every time before you bowl, and see that the fieldsmen are just where you want them. If you want them to move, tell 'em so. Or if you are shy, and do not like doing it yourself, get the captain to do it. No good captain will mind taking a suggestion. You are both working together for the good of the side, don't forget.

If a man's defence is too good, and you cannot get through it, try bowling slightly short and just outside the off stump. You may induce him to give the slips a chance. If he will not nibble, give him an over or two of it, and suddenly slam one in straight and well pitched up. You may catch him unawares. Try schemes like this the whole time. Brains do tell. A chess-player has to think a good many moves ahead. So does a cricketer, especially a bowler. A batsman may have a pet stroke—a cut past third man, for example. If you have a real command of length and direction, you have several courses of action open to you. You can feed that stroke until he gets careless and lifts one. Or you can starve that same stroke until he is so unused to it that the unexpectedness of it, when it comes, will cause him to be lacking in judgment for the moment. And so he will be lost.

REMEMBER: A bowler must use his brains. He must *think* about every ball he bowls. A chap who just dishes up the same sort of stuff, ball after ball, is not much good—except to give the real bowlers a rest. He is what is called "an ordinary up-and-downer." The only effect he has is to play the batsmen in. There are a thousand and one plans you can make, and traps you can lay for the unwary batsman.

NOTE: A good wicket-keeper can help you a lot. It is well worth while having a bit of practice alone with the wicket-keeper of your team. Get him thoroughly used to every sort of ball that you can bowl.

NOTE: If you can get your worn-out and suffering pal to bat at the same time, it will be doubly useful; because the wicket-keeper's sight of the ball is quite different, if no batsman is there. The batsman's burly, great body makes rather a difference. The gentle wicket-keeper, if no one is obstructing his view, has a clear sight of the ball. Whereas, if a large human screen cuts off his view, he has to judge where the ball will go. That means practice for him, and for you. And it's a great thing to feel fairly sure that, if the batsman just snicks that favourite ball of yours that goes away a bit, you can be almost certain that the wicket-keeper will stick on to the chance, and not let you down. But only practice will do it.

If you spot that a fellow is keen on playing forward, right—you lure him on. Pitch them up to him. If, by practice, you can shorten your length a fraction, little by little, without showing it, you will draw him out farther and farther. His back foot will slide over the crease. Wallop go the bails. An agonized yell from the wicket-keeper, and up goes the umpire's finger. If, in the above case, the batsman connects, you have a decent chance of bringing off a caught-and-bowled.

Many a bowler has, like the North-West Mounted Police, "got his man" by the leg-before-wicket route. If you can bowl a ball on the middle and going away a bit to the off, you will have the batsman coming across to defend his off peg. All at once you pop in a ball which looks as if it is going to do the same. But you have not really turned your wrist or twisted your fingers. Result—it comes through straight. A dull hollow sound on his pads—and another good man gone west!

I recently umpired a Preparatory School match in which a youngster got a good batsman out by pure brain power. Needless to say, he had a good command of length. In fact, for a boy of thirteen, it was quite remarkable. He pitched well up for a couple of overs, and got his man playing well forward—incidentally taking a lot of punishment. Quite unexpectedly he pushed a slower one up about a couple of feet shorter, all with the same action. The batsman fell for it. Forward he went, and the bowler got a well-deserved, and very simple, caught and bowled.

One approaches the question of the googly with a certain amount of reserve. So many try it, but "few are chosen." It is not everybody's meat by a long chalk. Also, it is no good if you lose your length through it. Still, there are some freaks to whom it seems to come naturally. So we will just have a word or two about it. The off-break with a leg-break action is the real "wrong 'un." You will have to exercise your wrist so well that you can bend it over so much that the ball leaves your hand over the little finger. Sounds difficult—but not impossible. It is worth trying; but you will find that you will have to try a lot before it comes.

The story goes that the googly was invented by a girl! I don't know if this is true or not. Anyway, they say that Bosanquet was playing stump cricket with his sister. She noticed that a tennis-ball, bowled with a great deal of spin over the little finger, tended to come in from the *off*. So B. J. T. Bosanquet had a go at it. After trying it with a tennis-ball, he found that he could get the same results with a cricket ball. So he practised it like billy-oh, and suddenly burst on the cricket world, and created a sensation. At first he was just an ordinary fast bowler. One hopes that this is a true yarn!

TRY THIS: If you want to google eventually, spend a few minutes, several times a day, twisting the wrist round and round, so that the tips of the fingers make a complete circle. This will exercise those muscles that you will need to strengthen to bowl the googly. Ask Clarence Grimmett. Finger spin will not make a ball break so much as a wrist action. But it will make a faster ball turn a bit.

TRY THIS: To strengthen those fingers, take a ball in them, and spin it both ways, i.e., from left to right, and vice versa, every day for a few minutes. In the end you will find that, besides being able to spin the ball considerably, you will be able to control the spin.

REMEMBER: It is better to pitch up to the batsman than bowl short. A short 'un gives him too much time to think. He has plenty of time to cut on the off, or pull to leg. Even a half-volley is better than that. So many fellows nowadays seem scared of half-volleys that you may get him caught off one!

There is an exception to this rule, though. In a Test Match a bowler bowled the rankest of long hops to that prince of footwork experts, C. G. Macartney—the "Governor"—of Australia. Even that wily bird fell for it. He tried a wild sweep to leg; but the ball was on the wicket. He missed it, and was clean bowled!

Lastly, never mind being knocked about. Bide your time, and do not get rattled. So many bowlers, if hit, start bowling short. Do not do it. Keep pitching up to that batsman. Always keep on trying something, and you will catch him napping in the end.

The next bit is about Fielding.

FIFTH WICKET

Fielding: Lots of It

Fielding is the greatest fun in cricket. After all, it is the only full-time job in the game. Unless, of course, you "carry your bat" in both innings. W. G. Grace did that once, and was on the field while every ball in a three days' match was bowled. We are not all W. G.'s, though. If you notch a blob, you can always be sure of getting a bit of fielding. Even if you are not a bowler, you can always be on your toes in the field during off periods. Every ball has to be watched. And don't forget that you must back up the bowler. He depends on you. So you can't let him down. How would you like it yourself if you were a bowler, and, after scheming to get a batsman caught, you succeed in making him put one up, only to see that wretched fieldsman put it down again?

Remember: To be able to field well is to enjoy it. This cannot be done without tons of practice. A chap may make a century, and give it away again by slack fielding. Do you know that Jack Hobbs nearly lost his place, as a youngster, in the Surrey team because of his poor fielding? What did he do about it? He just practised and practised until he made himself into the best cover-point in Cricket, so that if a stroke went anywhere near him, you heard a pair of "Noes" from the batsmen.

You would be surprised if you could see the amount of practice put in by even first-class cricketers. That dashing pick-up and return to the wicket, and that beautifully judged long catch in the deep are not just natural or flukes. They've been tried out again and again until "practice has made perfect." Furthermore, one has to keep it up. What happens to brass if you don't keep it well polished? It soon goes all dull, doesn't it? So you have to keep your fielding polished up in the same way. Even a car engine has to be run pretty regularly to keep it in its best condition.

One of the best fieldsmen of modern times is A. P. F. Chapman, captain of Kent and England. He once made an amazing catch at the Oval. He was fielding in the "gully"—i.e., third man. He is an immense man, about six feet four inches, and weighing at least fourteen to fifteen stone. But he has trained himself to move with remarkable swiftness and agility. A fastish bowler was bowling and, by pitching a little short, made the ball get up a bit outside the off stump. The batsman got on top of one and cut it down hard. It went like a streak of lightning straight down towards Chapman's ankle. The latter made a sudden dive down and, with both hands, grabbed the ball, almost on the ground. But the force of the stroke knocked him right off his perch. He turned a complete somersault and landed with a thump on his back. They say the shock shook several of the pictures off the wall in the pavilion! One can't be quite certain of this, though! Anyway, he kept the ball up, which

FIFTH WICKET

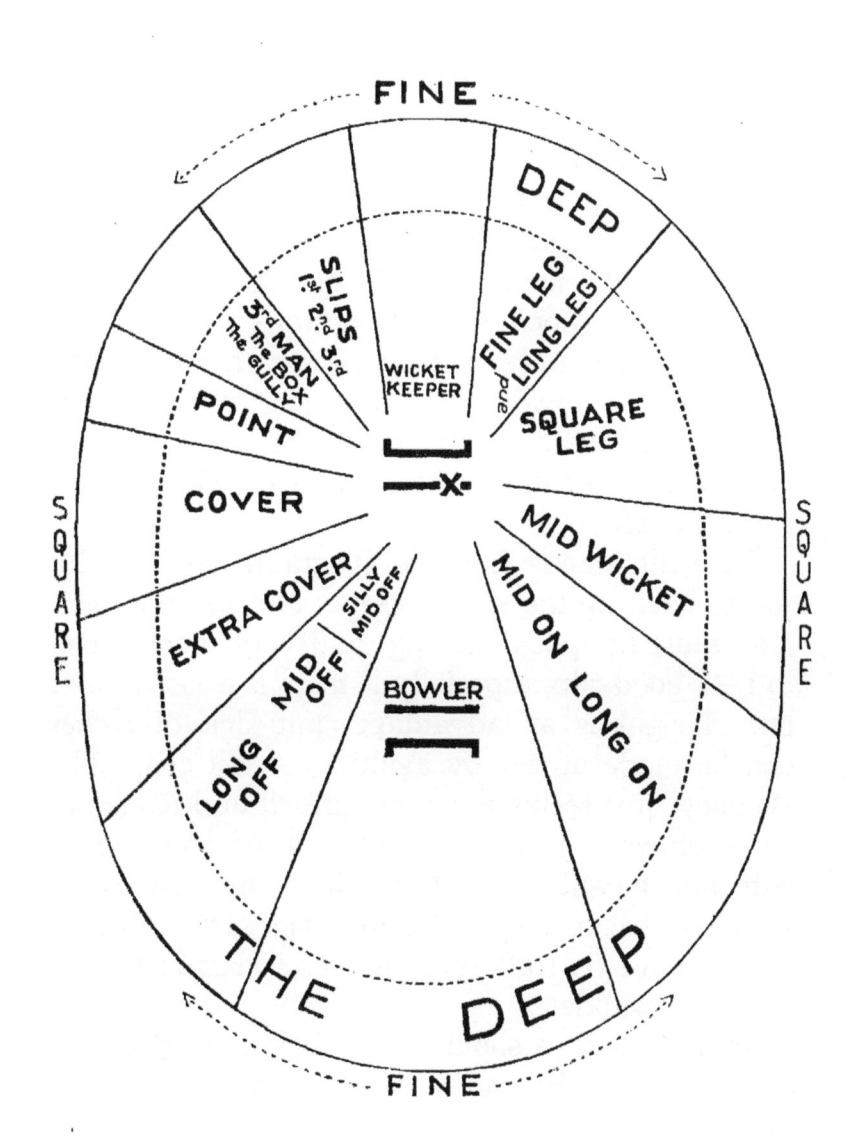

was the main thing. That catch was no fluke by any means. It was the outcome of tons of training.

Most fellows specialize in a certain position.

NOTE: It is as well to make yourself acquainted with other positions in the field than those that suit you best. You never know—if one of your side goes down for any reason, you may have to take his place at a moment's notice. So let us take the positions one by one. (Look at the Diagram.)

SLIPS: Generally a slow bowler has one slip. Medium-paced two slips. The fast merchant has three, called first, second and third slip. In extreme cases a fourth slip has been known. This is a bit rare, though.

First slip stands fine (see Diagram), and it is his job to back up the wicket-keeper and so save byes. You must be quick moving, and very much alive, to be a good slip, especially if there is a fast bowler on. Height is an advantage, but lack of inches can be made up for by agility. A tall chap, like Woolley, just seems to uncoil himself and reach out yards either way to grab up the unconsidered trifle with nonchalant ease. But a little 'un, like Patsy Hendren, has to keep on his toes, and move quickly. And doesn't he shift speedily, too? His feet seem fairly to twinkle.

NOTE: All slips should keep their eyes glued on the ball from the moment it leaves the bowler's hand.

A rather gruesome, but, I'm afraid, somewhat common, sight is that of a slip, when a chance comes towards him low down, flinging both arms and legs outwards like a Russian ballet dancer, or an animated Catherine wheel, and making a wild dash forward at the last moment. Always too late, of course. *No!* A thousand times better to take a quick step or two forward, and get the ball knee-high.

The slip-catching machine is an excellent gadget. It is a sort of cradle affair, with well polished strips of wood formed in curves so that they make a kind of hollow, the top ones each side being straight. A couple of fellows stand at each end of it, about five yards away. When one of them hurls the ball on to the wooden strips, it comes off at a good pace. If the ball is thrown so that it strikes fairly far up on either side, it will need watching, as enough spin is imparted to it to make catching fairly difficult.

REMEMBER: A ball coming to you from this position is edged by the bat, and so will tend to swerve to the *left*. Always be prepared for this. The best position to stand in is (a) with the feet apart, so as to be able to cover more ground to the right or left, (b) on the toes, in order to get into action quickly, (c) crouching forward, in which case you will be more likely to get one that pitches a bit short.

NOTE: If one of the slips has to return the ball to the bowler, he should always send a high, slow catch that comes to the bowler waist-high. This is easy for him to take, and saves the hard-working fellow from wasting his energy in having to stoop down, which is a tiring business and which should be wholly unnecessary. Some bowlers, notably

Voce and Tate, have reduced the feat of kicking up a rolling ball with their boots and catching it to a fine art. This is not done for effect. There is sound common sense behind it. It is in case a fieldsman returns the ball carelessly. Then that unnecessarily tiring stoop can be avoided.

As a matter of fact, it would be as well to chuck the ball to the wicket-keeper and let him do the return to the bowler. After all, he gets any amount of practice at it and should be fairly expert.

THIRD MAN: He is a sort of outer slip. He stands about half-way between slips and point. This position is nicknamed "The Gully" or "The Box." I do not know why, but there it is. Third man also has to keep his eye on the ball from the second it leaves the bowler's hand. For a slow bowler, third man stands fairly near in. For a fast bowler deeper, so that he can snap up that shot that the batsman fondly hoped would be a nice late cut, but which he managed to put up in the air.

Third man must be nippy on his feet and ready to dash madly in all directions! He often has to run like blazes to save a boundary.

NOTE: In common with all other fieldsmen, third man *must* chase the ball right up to the boundary. It's horrible to see the field standing still and watching a ball careering away, as though they had little interest in its progress. You never know—the hundredth chance of cutting off a boundary may come off.

REMEMBER: It's just as important to save a run as to make it.

POINT is fast disappearing from cricket. The swerving bowler is making him rather useless. It is a most difficult place to field in, because the ball always has a left spin on. Point should watch the bat and not the bowler.

The fade-out of point is rather a pity. They say that W. G. Grace used to perform miracles in this position.

COVER really means cover-point. He has to sprint for what point misses. As the cut-drive comes to cover, he has to watch out for that left-hand twist. Cover should stand on his toes, and, as the bowler is taking his run, he should move a pace or two towards the batsman, so that he can dash in to the short one.

Covers have been responsible for more "run outs" than most fieldsmen. This is mostly because batsmen try to steal singles from them. An off stroke is easy to judge and see, because it leaves the batsman from in front of him.

The classic example of a cover-point is J. B. Hobbs. He made himself into such a batsman's nightmare that, when a ball went anywhere within his reach, the discordant duet of *"No!"* could be heard at the top of the Oval gasometer!

Next we come to:

EXTRA-COVER—if there is one. His job is the same as cover's. He stands between cover and mid-off.

MID-OFF is between extra-cover and the bowler. He has to stop straight drives, so he must have a good pair of hands and plenty of pluck. He also should take a step or two towards the batsman as the bowler bowls. A slow bowler should have a LONG-OFF. He stands behind mid-off, "out in the deep," nearer the boundary.

NOTE: Cover, extra-cover, mid-on and mid-off must keep their eyes on the bat while the bowler is bowling, so that they can anticipate what shot the batsman is shaping for.

REMEMBER: If fielding in the deep, that is, away from the wicket and near the boundary, you must practise long catches, picking up quickly and throwing in. The ideal throw-in bounces once and comes to the bowler or wicket-keeper in line with the top of the wickets, so that with a sideways sweep they can send the bails flying. Gregory, of Surrey, and Don Bradman are expert throwers-in. Both of them will tell you that it is only by any amount of practice that they have been able to run so many men out.

Pity the poor wicket-keeper when the ball comes in along the ground or on the half-volley. He has to bend right down, and can hardly be sprightly in that posture. It doesn't give a chap a chance, does it? And it's worse still for the bowler. After all, the wicket-keeper is wearing gloves, and the bowler's finger-tips are not made of cast-iron.

MID-ON. Has the same job to leg as mid-off has on the other side of the bowler. There may also be a long-on in the deep.

There used to be a sort of legend that mid-on was an easy place to field in. So any dud fielder there was on the side was dispatched there to be out of

"SLIPS"

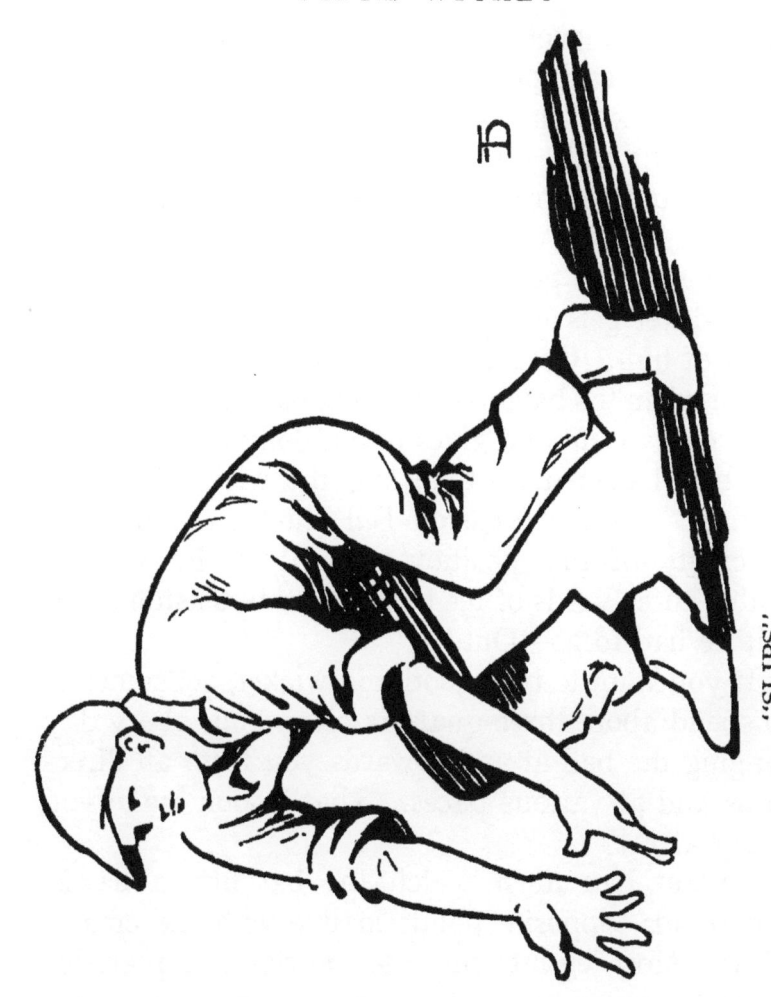

Note.—Hands just about to close on the ball

the way. No such thing, and don't you believe it. There is no easy position in fielding.

MID-WICKET has a very unenviable, but most important, task nowadays. He stands between mid-on and square-leg. He gets tons of kicks and precious few ha'pence. When a batsman slightly pulls a shot, he gets all his weight into it. Result—mid-wicket gets it, not exactly in the neck, but in front of him. On the other hand, his ha'pence consist of when the batsman, playing back to a swerving ball, cocks it up and gives him a dolly catch. Even the best batsmen do this, and the wicket is worth getting. On one occasion Bill Hitch, who made a speciality of this position, caught P. F. Warner within three yards of his bat. Plum was astonished, but he had to go—Out!

If you want to be a good mid-wicket, get someone to spend about three-quarters of an hour every day flinging the ball at and towards you from all directions and at various paces. That'll soon make you fairly alert!

SQUARE-LEG must watch the bat like a hawk. He stands, opposite point, in line with the crease. NOTE: Most leg hits curve to the right. Square-leg should always be ready to run back, in case the batsman lifts one over his head.

LONG-LEG: Position is opposite third man. Once again he will find that the ball, coming from the edge of the bat, will break towards his right hand.

FINE-LEG is a sort of leg-side slip. He and long-leg should watch the ball all the way down the pitch from the bowler's hand.

"ZAAAAAT!"
Georgie Duckworth—no more words needed

[*Keystone View Company*

HAMMOND JUST GETS HOME

Why? Because he slid his bat along edgewise. But Oldfield took the ball beautifully

REMEMBER ONCE MORE: Slip and fine-legs should watch the ball with the same concentration that the batsman does. The rest of the fieldsmen watch the bat. In other words: In front of the wicket, eye on bat. Behind the wicket, eye on ball.

REMEMBER: All fieldsmen must be on the alert for every ball. Nothing looks worse, or gives a batsman more confidence, than a slack field. It also takes the heart out of a bowler. He is never sure whether runs won't be given away, or catches dropped. So he just thinks: "Well, what's the use?" and bowls badly as a consequence.

Never stand with your hands in your pockets. It doesn't look workmanlike.

NOTE: Backing up to save an over-throw is absolutely necessary. The nearest fieldsman *must* get behind the bowler or wicket-keeper, at a distance of ten to fifteen yards, in case the throw is a bad one.

Throwing-in should be practised regularly. If fielding far from the wicket, you must be able to take a high, long catch, or to pick up a rolling ball quickly and throw in just as quickly. These throws cannot be practised enough.

REMEMBER: A ball that pitches half-volley at a fellow's feet is worse than useless. For one thing, it is hard to stop. For another, even if stopped, it is most difficult to get it on to the wicket.

Some fieldsmen make themselves so efficient that they can stop a ball one-handed and slightly behind them. Then they can sweep that ball towards the wicket without wasting time.

REMEMBER: Time is pretty important. A fast runner can run ten yards in a second!

This pick-up and throw-in looks as though it was all the same movement. G. L. Jessop, the big hitter, was marvellous at it. He used to field at cover or extra-cover, and turn himself sideways as the ball came, so that his left shoulder was pointing towards the target wicket. He would take the hardest drives in this position, that is, well behind him, and have the ball back at the wicket like greased lightning. He used to return a low ball with a below-the-shoulder throw, so as not to waste time straightening up. You've got a long way to go before you can reach Jessop's proficiency at it. But it's an ideal worth striving for.

BOWLERS AND WICKET-KEEPERS: Be like Mrs. Micawber, and "never desert the" wicket. If you prance about all over the field, one of two things will happen: (a) you will not be there to take the return and run out the batsman who is sneaking short ones; (b) you will get in somebody's light and make him make a muck of it.

If a catch goes between two or more fieldsmen—who all feel an itch to go for it, naturally—listen for your captain's stentorian tones. If he yells the name of one of you, t'others *must* stop dead at once. After all, what does it matter who makes the catch so long as the batsman gets his marching orders?

This next bit is worth repeating.

How often have you seen a fieldsman, when a catch comes towards him, wildly fling his arms out in all directions, take a step backwards, and then,

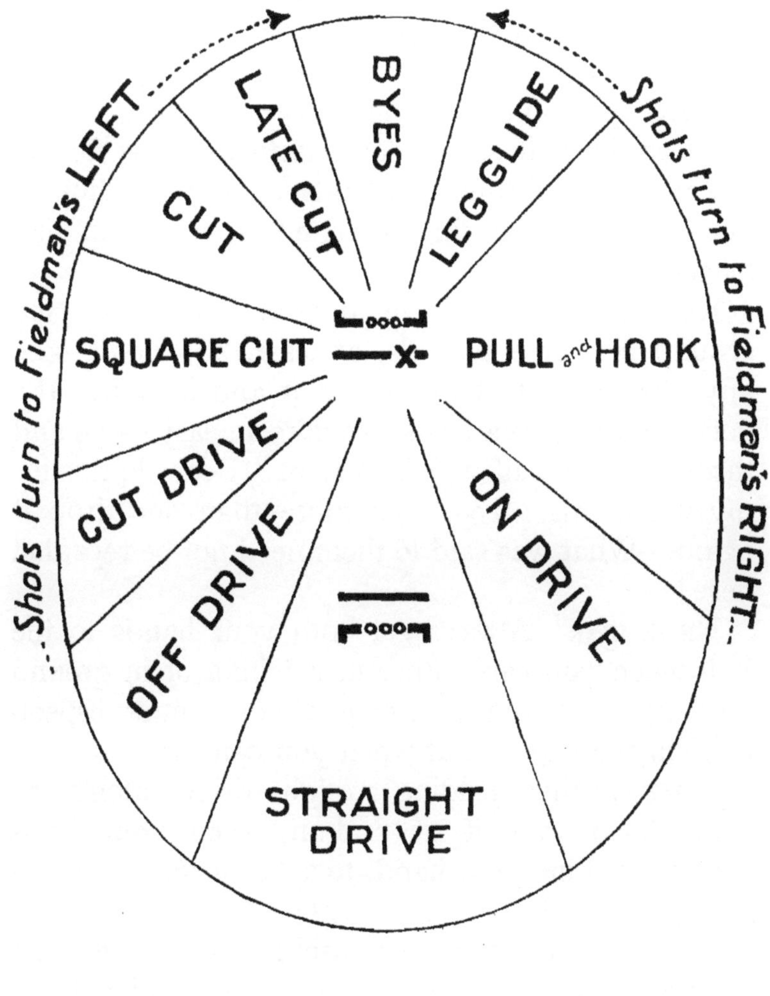

...Shots turn to Fieldman's LEFT...
...Shots turn to Fieldman's RIGHT...
BYES
LATE CUT
LEG GLIDE
CUT
SQUARE CUT
PULL and HOOK
CUT DRIVE
OFF DRIVE
ON DRIVE
STRAIGHT DRIVE

too late, lunge forward and miss the catch? Often, I'll be bound. Well, please *do not do it*. Cut it out of your programme. Stand on your toes and go forward every time. You can always jump to it if it is going higher than you thought.

NOTE: The best way to catch is to hold your hands slightly apart and pointing away from you. Close them as the ball comes down until the little fingers are crossing. As the ball lands, cross your thumbs over it, curl your fingers round it, and grip like blazes.

REMEMBER: You have to hold the ball off the ground for three seconds, at least. So don't take any chances. Just bite on to it and *hold* it. It's very pretty to see a fieldsman take an easy catch and throw up the ball with a sort of "I-can-do-this-in-my-sleep" air. I've seen more than one drop it again. What was said to them need not be repeated here!

REMEMBER: Always get both your hands to the ball when you can, either in catching or in ground fielding. Sometimes, of course, you cannot, especially, in the slips. But when you can, do.

NOTE: When fielding straight drives along the ground, at mid-off or mid-on, keep your heels together behind your hands to act as a sort of second line of defence.

The field-out is a very useful form of fielding practice. It is rather good fun, too, and it helps you to improve your batting, bowling, and running between the wickets, as well as fielding. Besides, it gives everyone a chance of a knock, a couple of overs, a turn behind the wicket, and fielding in all positions.

REMEMBER: *Always* try for every chance, even if it looks hopeless. That difficult catch may stick, after all, and change the whole fortunes of the game. *Never* think: "Oh, I can't get that one." You might. And you'll kick yourself afterwards for not having tried.

REMEMBER: Finally and lastly, and it cannot be repeated too often, be a live wire in the field. On your toes for every ball.

Now for that rather special fieldsman—the wicket-keeper.

SIXTH WICKET

Keeping Wicket

THE wicket-keeper has the most interesting job of the lot. He has to concentrate the whole of the time on every ball. So he sees more of the game than any other fieldsman.

In a Test Match during the recent (1936-37) tour in Australia, W. A. Oldfield "kept" for Australia and Leslie Ames for England. "Believe it or not," but in the course of the match over a thousand runs were scored, and the number of byes let by these two gallants between them was—one! Pretty good concentration, that!

NOTE: It is a good idea to relax between balls. As the bowler is walking back to his "take-off," take a few steps round in a circle. This will bring you back fresh to your job. This applies to all *other* fieldsmen, too, by the way.

There is an old cricket saying: "Only a lunatic ever becomes a wicket-keeper." I would not go so far as to say that. Still, wicket-keepers are, somehow, different from other people. If you have a definite urge to stand behind the stumps and take any old thing that comes along, well and good, do so. If, contrariwise, you are not quite sure if you would like it or not, by all means have a shot at it. You may be born for the job, without knowing it. Give it a good try out, and then, if you feel that you are not having too good a time, or making a mess of it, drop it.

To be a good wicket-keeper, you need a safe pair of hands, quickness of movement—and a cool head.

NOTE: Don't be showy. The extra effort needed to show off is not really worth it. W. A. Oldfield is "Public Wicket-keeper No. 1." And he would scorn to resort to showmanship. He's just quiet, neat, and super-efficient. He makes no movement that is not absolutely necessary.

The best place to stand, when waiting for what the bowler has to offer, is behind the off stump. This is because the batsman's body is in the light to leg, so you will get a clearer view of the ball as it comes down the pitch. Also, most bowlers avoid bowling to leg, as a leg ball is, if at all wide or short, fairly easy to tonk. Some bowlers *do* attack the leg stump, of course. And left-handed bowlers find it their natural mark. So you will have made yourself used to taking leg balls as well.

Stand with your legs apart. Then move your left foot up to the right, and get across quickly to take anything wide on the off, or vice versa, you can come across with your right and bring yourself smartly into position to take a ball to leg. In the case of a ball on the off, you can, more or less, watch it all the way into your gloves. But a leg ball is hidden, for the later part of its journey, by a large and not very transparent body—that of that hulking brute of a batsman! All you can do is to watch the ball most intently until the view is shut off. Your gloves should, by now, be in such a position that the ball, if it misses batsman and bat, just plops gently but firmly into them. If the bat snicks it, you will have to move pretty rapidly in the last split second to readjust your position. All this is true if you are standing right up to the wicket. If you are standing back to the speed fiend, things will be easier, because you will have plenty of time, comparatively, to get into the right position after the ball has popped into view again from behind the batsman. This is one of the arguments for standing back. George Duckworth is a master at taking leg balls. He seems to have a "second sight" as to where the balls are going. Being rather diminutive in height, he often has to make a dive, both feet off the ground, for chances which a taller could just reach out and grab. But Duckworth "gets 'em" most times.

NOTE: Many young wicket-keepers fall into a fatal error of standing half-way—that is, about five yards from the wicket. This is a compromise, and is absolutely no use at all. Maybe they think it doesn't look brave to stand back. That's all rot. It is better either to be up where you can reach the wicket and make sure of stumpings and runs out, or stand right back where you can make a certainty of catches. Half-way (for ladies!) merely means that you can't touch the wicket and catches are more difficult.

REMEMBER: Try to be there before the ball reaches you. Do not be fussy or too dashing. Move quietly, but quickly. This will come with tons of practice. Some wicket-keepers like to bend down almost double while waiting for the ball. Others only crouch slightly forward. That is, of course, "to taste," as the cook says. Do whichever gives you the best sight of the ball.

The old-time wicket-keeper used to stand fairly upright. Gregor MacGregor was one of the finest 'keepers who ever played for England. He used to stand right up to the wicket to take the fastest bowling. And fast bowling *was* fast bowling in those days. Tom Richardson, who "on Cornstalk wickets played blue bungo with the ball," and Kortright were even faster than Larwood. But MacGregor made no bones about standing up to stuff like that. Nowadays the Ameses and the Oldfields squat a bit and stand back to the express ones. Still, they get just as good, if not better, results. So choose the way you like best.

NOTE: No part of you, not even the tip of your nose, may be in front of the wicket when you receive the ball. Otherwise all your frantic appeals for stumped, caught or run out will be answered by the umpire with a stony glare!

Watch the bowler's hand as he delivers the ball. It will give you some idea as to whether he is turning the ball or not; and, if he is, which way.

Have you noticed the number of wicket-keepers who are, or were, good batsmen as well? Taking a few names at random: Dick Lilley, MacGregor, Ames, H. B. Cameron, Oldfield all made centuries in Tests or first-class matches. Even Strudwick, of Surrey and England, made over ninety in a Gentlemen *v.* Players Match. And there are many stories of little Georgie Duckworth, whose agonized

"Zaaat?" is known the world over. He used to go in last for Lancashire. When his cheery little figure, padded and gloved, was seen coming down the pavilion steps, the fieldsmen used to start edging towards the gate with a sort of "Now it's all over" air. But Georgie had other ideas. Having boundless determination, he resolved that he would make himself into a batsman. And become a batsman he did. He practised, and practised, and practised. His team pals backed him up and coached him. Soon Georgie began making twenties, then thirties, and at last fifties and more. He will probably get a century one day. He is already uncommonly hard to shift, and is more than useful to have low down in the batting order. He often adds just that stiffening that is needed to make Lancashire's tail wag considerably.

You see, a wicket-keeper has a "front row at the stalls," so to speak. He can study how expert batsmen deal with the bowling. These methods can be "noted for future reference." Besides, the wicket-keeper is constantly having what is almost a "batsman's eye" view of the ball.

NOTE: Once more—try to get your hands into the position where you judge the ball will smack into them.

NOTE: *Never* "snatch." That is, do not push your gloves out at the last moment, try to take the ball, and pull them back again. It is wasted energy. If your hands are properly in position and the batsman has dragged his back foot over the crease, then the action of taking the ball and sweeping the bails off is all one and the same movement.

NOTE: If you have to push your gloves out, take the ball, and then bring it back to the bails, you have to go through three separate and distinct motions. Whereas, if you can have your gloves ready, and, the moment the ball crashes into them, convey it with extreme rapidity to the wicket, the whole job of work is practically one movement. So energy is not wasted, and time, which means everything, is saved. A tiny second means a tremendous lot in cricket.

REMEMBER: The above needs a terrible amount of trying out. But it pays. It is rather a joy when you cause that chap, who might have made a century, to go and cool his heels before he has really got set.

TRY THIS: Get your old pal to stand about half-way up the pitch at nets and throw them in at you just outside the off stump. Practise take-and-sweep every time until you have it. Now get him to bung them up on the leg. When you are fairly certain in that position, try and get him, if he is not quite worn out, to mix them up.

NOTE: The most difficult ball to take is one that pitches a bit short and comes in fairly high over the stumps. (Probably the batsman has been lured out by a shorter one and missed it.) It is hard to get the gloves into position for taking a ball going at one's chest. There are several ways of dealing with this awkward business: (a) You put your gloves pointing up, palms away, thumbs crossed behind, and shove the ball down hard on to the stumps, or close your hands round it and grip for a catch; (b) you can step to left or right and take it sideways, according to whether the ball is to leg or off. (This is not so good, as byes result from misses, which would be fairly frequent.)

If the ball is not high, about in line with the stomach, you can point the gloves downwards, forming a safe ledge for the ball to drop into after it has hit the heel of your hand. In the case of a catch, you can easily close your fingers upwards and over the ball. For a stumped or run out, you will have to force gloves forwards and downwards on to the bails. Not so easy; but possible with practice.

A little of this "every day and in every way" and you will soon get "better and better."

NOTE: Whenever possible, keep your gloves pointing away from you when shaping for the ball to land. There is an exception to this excellent rule which we will look into later. Even when the batsman connects and beats the ball properly, your job is nowhere finished. You must watch where the hit goes, and immediately place yourself so that the wicket is between you and the fieldsman who is dealing with it. There is such a thing as run out, you know. Running out is done in the same way as stumping.

REMEMBER: It is a golden rule never to desert your wicket. Still, Strudwick used to amuse the crowd by running almost to the boundary after a ball that had found a hole in the field. But he never did this unless he was perfectly sure of the teamwork of his side, and that someone would back him up and take his place at the wicket.

TRY THIS: Practise taking full-pitch throws-in from short range, putting the wicket down each time.

NOTE: From short range fieldsmen throw in full pitch. It saves time and is more accurate. REMEMBER, THOUGH, not all fieldsmen are accurate, so you will be wise to practise taking returns from all angles and at all heights. Your "dear old pal" can help you a lot here.

As regards catching, that is a question of your quickness of eye. After a lot of practice and experience, a first-class wicket-keeper can judge pretty well whether the batsman is going to touch the ball, and allow for the resulting deflection. Never leave anything to chance. Keep your eyes wide open and watch the ball right into your gloves.

REMEMBER AGAIN: *Never* leave your wicket. There is always a fieldsman near enough to a stroke to deal with it, without your butting in and messing him up. Besides, what is going to happen to the poor, lonely wicket after you have deserted it? True, another fieldsman can take your place, but he is not padded and gloved like you, and so is not fit to take a hard return.

NOTE: When taking a ball high and wide on the off, keep the left glove flat and pointing away, like an Egyptian dancer, and the right pointing up at right angles from it. The ball should then hit the palm of your right glove, and drop cosily into the left. Close the right over it, and grab it hard.

Reverse this for a ball wide on the leg—i.e., right glove flat, and left glove pointing up.

REMEMBER: Do not be scared of appealing. After all, you are in a position to know if you have made a catch or run a fellow out. But please do not appeal too much for leg before wicket, and do not appeal unless you are fairly certain the batsman is out. Too much appealing does not sound sporting and can be a rotten nuisance. Umpires are not exactly fond of it, either. Duckworth's squeak, of course, is well known. That is the outcome of super-keenness. But Georgie does not appeal without good reason.

Avoid unnecessary flourishes. A run out or a stumped are so often a case of a split second that, while you are doing your graceful act, the batsman has just that little extra moment in which to get home.

NOTE: If a batsman's toe or bat is only *on* the line, with the rest of him outside it, and you put the wicket down, he is definitely out. Some part of him, or his bat, must be *on* the ground and *over* the crease.

NOTE: If either or both bails are off, you will have to pull a stump out of the ground while holding the ball to get him out.

Finally, REMEMBER, think of the bowler. By that I mean, take great care how you return the ball to him. The poor chap has a lot of work to do, and wants to be carefully nursed. Do not add to his work. A return along the ground means that he will have to bend down and use up a great deal of energy that might be better employed. A half-volley that pitches at his feet is worse still. The ideal is a high slow catch which he can take waist high, or a slow first bounce that he can get without bending down. All this is well worth practising.

REMEMBER: Quietness and efficiency beat all the gallery work in the world. Gregor MacGregor of England, W. Oldfield of Australia, and the late H. B. Cameron of South Africa—probably the three greatest wicket-keepers who ever lived—never made an unnecessary movement.

And now, if you hope to be a captain, read on.

SEVENTH WICKET

Captaincy

WE cannot all be captains, of course. Still, one of the side must be the leader. A team without a captain would be like a body without a head—not much use. So I hope that those of you who are "rank and file" will back up your captain, and be thoroughly loyal to him. You may think you know better than he does. It may seem to you, at times, that he is going all wrong. But it does not matter. Do not grouse about it. By all means go up to him in the "I say, old chap" spirit, and make a suggestion. No real captain will mind that. After all, his is not an enviable job by any means. He is responsible, and he will be blamed if things go wrong, not you.

A captain's most important job is on the field. Watch your fieldsmen like a hawk. Glance round before every ball to see that no one has strayed out of his place.

NOTE: If a batsman has found a hole in the field, put a man there and block it.

For some reason or other, Australian captains nowadays seem to be cleverer at this than ours. Bradman, of course, is a tough proposition. He can, apparently, beat a ball past third man and immediately afterwards, despatch an identical ball through mid-off. His most baffling stroke is a sort of half-hook, half on-drive, which may travel in any direction between mid-on and near square-leg. As he hits with almost complete accuracy, he is enough to turn any captain's hair grey.

REMEMBER: Do not let your team get rattled. If the other side is knocking your bowling about, change your bowlers frequently. Nothing unsettles a batsman so much as constant changes. He has to readjust himself each time. It is a good idea, when their star batsman comes in, to give him a few changes straightaway at the beginning of his innings.

Study your bowlers. Do not tire them out, even if they are getting wickets. A few short spells are better than one long, wearying plug. If you are stumped for an idea, never mind going to your vice-captain and asking his advice. Two heads are so often better than one. Do not be pig-headed about it and think it is beneath your dignity. That is merely silly.

Many a captain in Test and County Matches has consulted with an experienced professional as to his course of action. Rhodes, Hobbs (who once actually captained England), Sutcliffe and Hammond have been of the greatest service to their respective captains.

REMEMBER: Take first knock if you win the toss—unless the wicket is really bad. There is a sort of mistaken idea among very young cricketers that it is a "Good thing" (1066 and all that!) to know how many runs you have to make to win. As a matter of fact, it isn't. If any of your side are at all subject

G

to "nerves," that complaint will only be increased by such knowledge.

In *Tom Brown's Schooldays* we read that Tom, as captain of the eleven, after winning the toss on a perfect wicket, "with the usual liberality of young hands," put the M.C.C. in to bat. The M.C.C.! I ask you! That, to my mind, is the only blemish in a really magnificent school yarn.

An England captain once put Australia in to bat on a wicket that looked to be difficult. Macartney made a century before lunch, and Australia finished, at close of play, with some four hundred and odd for a couple of wickets. So, putting your opponents in is a tricky business.

NOTE: There are three main types of wicket:

(a) Good, hard and dry—in which case bat first.

(b) Wet, with no sun, and easy (i.e., it will not take spin and slows down fast stuff)—in which case bat first.

(c) Wet, with the sun shining hard on it (difficult, because the ball will turn a lot, and fast bowling will be apt to pop up at awkward angles)—in which case you can risk putting the other side in first. Besides, it will probably be drier and easier by the time you have to bat.

If one of your fieldsmen drops a catch, even if it is a sitter, do not cuss or nag at him. Just say, "Hard lines, old chap," or "Well tried." It will buck him up no end. I have seen perfectly good fieldsmen put off for a whole game because they had the bad luck to put an easy one on the carpet early on, and the captain has yelled at them for it.

There are two ways of being a captain—a right way and a wrong way. The right way is by encouragement and setting a good example. The wrong way is by nagging. All the great captains in cricket, from P. F. Warner, of England, to

LISTEN TO YOUR CAPTAIN!

H. L. Collins, of Australia, have been quiet, almost reserved, men, who inspired confidence in their men by a complete lack of fussiness.

NOTE: If two or more fieldsmen are going for a ball, you must shout out loud the name of the one whose ball you judge it is. Insist that the others stop dead at once. This is well worth practising.

A case of this last happened in Australia lately. Bradman played a bit too soon, and skied a ball straight up in the air. First slip, fine leg and Ames, the wicket-keeper, all went for it, as it was about equidistant from all three of them. Now Bradman's wicket is about the hardest to get in the world. So no chance could be refused. "Gubby" Allen called Ames's name. The other two froze in their tracks, and the catch was made. If discipline hadn't been pretty good, there would have been a three-fold collision—and Bradman would have grinned and carried on with his innings.

REMEMBER: *Always* encourage, *never* curse. If a fellow makes a bloomer, then sympathize with him. It may be your turn next. If you make a mistake yourself, the chap you have gone for will not think much of you. But if you have sympathized with him, he will be much more likely to make allowances himself.

NOTE: You must insist on discipline all the same. This can be done quietly, though. If you appeal to a real cricketer's better nature, he will never let you down. Now and again, of course, you may find a black sheep—that is, a chap who is a nuisance, and thinks he knows better. If you do come across such a plague-spot, drop him from the team like hot coal.

Every team should have one comic chap on board. He can keep the crew cheery and happy; and a team like that is welcomed anywhere, and is a delight to play against. When things are going wrong, your comedian can often raise drooping spirits, and the team will play with a better heart. The London Cockney, with his priceless sense of humour, was one of the reasons for our winning the Great War, where team work mattered more than anything.

The funny fellow, if he has tact as well, will always take away the bitterness of defeat from his own side, as well as the others.

NOTE THOUGH: It is your job, as captain, to see that genuine fun doesn't go too far, and degenerate into mere stupid ragging. There is a medium in all things.

I shall have a few words to say about cricket comedians in the "Tenth Wicket."

NOTE: Above all, encourage your chaps by example. Always be all out and full of enthusiasm yourself. Nothing is so catching as enthusiasm. Infect your team with it. Never slack off yourself. The best type of officer or non-commissioned officer in the Army or Air Force, or rank or rating in the Navy, is he who never tells a man to do what he cannot do himself. You will find your men will back you up all right.

Now we come to a rather tender point. Some coaches like to umpire matches, especially in schools, and captain the side themselves from that position of trust. I am utterly against this practice. Coaching should be done, and advice given, before and after matches. How can a boy be expected to learn to captain a team if it is always done for him?

It is only by his mistakes that he learns. These should be pointed out afterwards. You will never get self-reliance by not allowing a captain to "hoe his own row."

I have also seen school matches "captained" (and very badly sometimes) from the pavilion. This is wrong, wrong, utterly wrong. There is such a thing as being *too* keen to win.

Sometimes you will meet an opposing captain who will try to get his own way by means of a loud voice and boisterous manner. You know the sort of thing: "Heads! Splendid! You have won the toss. That means you will put us in, of course. Good! Come on, chaps. Shove your pads on. We are batting." Do not fall for that sort of stuff. Be quiet and gentle with him. Just take it as a joke. But do not give way to him.

NOTE: The hardest job is that of a captain who is also a bowler. He does not like to put himself on. Or, in some cases, he bowls too much. Well, that must be left to your own good sense. Do not be scared of putting yourself on, or keeping yourself on—if you are taking wickets. But please do not grab all the bowling if you are not being effective. It looks greedy and selfish.

Perhaps the ideal position for a captain is at the wicket. He has the best idea of whether the bowler is being troublesome and likely to get wickets or not. Also, he is in a central position—always a good position, as he can sign to the fieldsmen instead of having to shout. The only disadvantage is that he

FIELDING—AN ALL-TIME JOB
He doesn't look very pretty, does he?

can't see what's going on behind him in the slips or at fine leg.

Study your fieldsmen. It isn't always necessary for point and mid-on, or square-leg and mid-off to change places, or for long-off and long-leg to do ditto at the end of the over, for instance. If you can save them any unnecessary trouble, always do so.

Changing the field for a left-hander should also be studied thoroughly. Mid-on becomes mid-off, etc. This saves time, and unneeded fussing about in the field. You should have a sort of mental photograph in your head of all the positions.

REMEMBER: Be sporting. Do not crow if you win. Do not grouse if you lose—congratulate the other fellows. "Topping game. Thoroughly enjoyed it," should be your first words, win or lose.

NOTE: If there is a possible chance of getting runs, tell your batsmen to go bald-headed for them, even at the risk of losing their wickets and the match. A loss through a real sporting effort to hit off the runs is worth a ton of drawn games or runaway victories. After all, if you have had a good, exciting and enjoyable game, the result does not matter so very much.

REMEMBER: If you have a fast bowler, and the wicket is at all dangerous, take him off. You would not like it much if you were one of the opposing batsmen yourself, would you? No match is worth winning by laying the other fellows out.

Finally and lastly, see that your team behaves itself. Do not let the non-batters fool about and make a row. It gives a visiting team, who are, naturally, on their best behaviour, a bad impression. By all means crack a few jokes on the field between wickets, but, the moment "man-in" has sounded, discourage skylarking. And sit heavily on the pest who tries to argue with the umpire.

And so the next wicket.

EIGHTH WICKET
PRACTICE AND HOW TO LIVE

CRICKET is one of those games, like billiards, that look so easy when played by the expert. A nonchalant drive past cover, a careless-looking step forward in the slips to take what seems an ordinary catch, just a little flick of the wrist and that slow, tossed-up ball fizzes off the pitch and takes the off-stump—it all looks so simple. *But*—and it is a very big *but* indeed—no one has made good at this greatest of all Games without hours and hours, and then more hours, of *practice*. Nets, field-outs, fielding practice, all these have gone to make the greatest cricketers. Even men with the natural genius of W. G. Grace, Jack Hobbs or Don Bradman, and hundreds of others, have to keep themselves constantly in trim. Those beautiful flowing drives, cuts and glances that Woolley does to perfection were not attained without a good gruelling at the nets. And isn't it worth it? What, to a batsman, can compare with the thrill of a perfect off-drive speeding to the boundary? Think of the deep-rooted satisfaction of the bowler when, after a tense duel with the batsman, he sees a stump lying flat. There is the glorious feeling of the fieldsman who, by perfect judgment, gets to a catch that everyone thought was only half a chance, and holds it. But think also of the long, long training which has made these things possible.

NOTE: When batting at nets, please do not treat it as a time in which to indulge in happy-go-lucky slogging. You will only get into bad habits. And a bad habit is so easy to acquire, yet so difficult to drop. Open your shoulders, by all means, to your favourite shots, but also concentrate on strengthening weak ones.

No cricketer worth his salt would ever grudge the time spent in improving himself. The ultimate object—to be good at the greatest of games—is worth any sacrifice.

REMEMBER: If you are lucky enough to have a good coach, listen to what he says. You do not really know better than he does, however much you may think you do. After all, his experience is probably longer and wider than yours. He is bound to know a little bit about what is good, or bad, for you.

NOTE: It is at nets that the bowler gets his real chance to improve his length.

ALSO NOTE: All nets should have a whitewashed mark of some sort put down where a good length ball ought to pitch. But do not forget that you will have to vary your length according to whether the batsman is tall or short.

REMEMBER: Constant fielding practice is absolutely necessary. There is no department of the game in which it is so easy to get out of touch. It is no good hitting fours if you are going to give them all away again in the field. The FIELD OUT is a most useful type of practice. Thirteen fellows are needed —two to bat, and the rest to field as a full side. Each pair of batsmen has about four overs' knock. Everyone has a turn at bowling. As many as possible should have a turn behind the wicket. Pads and gloves are not wanted. They only waste time.

An occasional tip-and-run is not a bad idea. It is good fun, and teaches you when to steal short runs—and when not to.

REMEMBER: Any hit in front of a line drawn between point and mid-wicket is definitely the hitter's call. Anything behind that line, and byes, are the call of the fellow at the other end.

NOTE: Always run the first run *hard*. After that, use your judgment. It may sound kiddish, but stump cricket with a tennis ball is not at all a bad scheme occasionally—especially to teach you how to drive. If you can drive a tennis ball cleanly on the half-volley really hard with a stump, you will find that it will help you a lot in the real thing.

Now a few words on How to Live. A cricketer must be physically fit, as much as any other sportsman. Anything slightly wrong with your body affects your eye, and you will play inside that half-volley. Result—tragedy! A bowler has to be ready to stand up to long spells of bowling, if necessary. That means stamina. And that means a fit body.

A fieldsman's eye and judgment have to be topnotch all the time, or that snap-catch, that means so much, will go astray.

About keeping fit:

NOTE: (a) Avoid late nights. Always be sure of getting your good eight hours in bed. Nothing puts your body out of tune so much as lack of proper rest. After all, it is at night that you put back into yourself all the energy that you have used up during the day. The old Australian rhyme of:

> "Eight hours' work,
> Eight hours' play,
> Eight hours' sleep, and
> Eight bob a day"

has sound common sense behind it.

REMEMBER: Do not read in bed. It is rotten for the eyes. Go to sleep straightaway.

NOTE: (b) Eat sensibly. Your clearness of eye depends a good deal upon your "tummy." If that useful organ is out of gear, you will have several "blind spots" instead of one!

I'll try to explain the "blind spot." At the back of your eye there is a kind of mirror called the retina. A gadget, entitled the optic nerve, carries the picture from the retina to your brain. So you are able to see. But, just where that optic nerve joins on to the jolly old retina, there is one little space from which no picture can come. If you look at a large dot a couple of yards away, and shift your eye slowly about, you will find a position where that dot will disappear. That is your "blind spot." If a bowler happens to pitch a ball so that its contact with the ground coincides with this "blind spot," I am afraid that, barring luck, you are "for it."

A bad digestion, caused by silly feeding, makes other spots in front of the eyes, and you will be at a double disadvantage.

Never rush your meals if you can help it. Chew your food well, so that the digestive juices will have a chance to get to work properly. If you swallow large lumps, those juices will go on strike, and you will have masses of food rotting inside you, and forming poisons. Always have a short rest after every meal. It helps the digestion.

Never eat late at night. If you go to sleep with a whole lot of stuff in your "innards," it stands to reason that you cannot digest it. Besides, you will probably have rotten nightmares. Imagine dreaming that you are batting with a toothpick against a gigantic Larwood, bowling with a huge crimson football! "No, no, a thousand times no!" Your last "eats" should be at least an hour before you retire to your little cot.

NOTE: (c) Cut out your smoking and drinking as much as possible. (This is for older fellows, of course. Youngsters would not think of it.) Both, or either, will get you down in the end. Smoking is bad for the eyes, and drinking saps your strength. They buck you up for a moment or two, but leave you worse off than you were before.

NOTE: (d) As soon as you get up in the morning, go to an open window and take a dozen deep breaths, breathing in through the nose, and out through the mouth. Press your hands against your lower ribs as you breathe out. This empties the lungs of used-up air, and lets clean, fresh air fill them. This will clear the fugginess out of you.

REMEMBER: *Always* lead a *regular* life. Get used to going to bed at the same time every night. It is easy to wake when you want to. Just tap your head on the pillow seven times before going to sleep. You will find that you will wake up at seven o'clock to the tick.

To touch on a rather unpleasant, but very important, subject—get into the habit of doing your business at the same time every morning, preferably as early as possible. Then the beastly stuff inside will have no chance of mucking about inside you and doing harm.

Here is a good way of spending a day:

7.0 a.m. Up with a bang, and breathing exercises.

7.15 a.m. Cold bath.

8.0 a.m. Breakfast . . . rest . . . and business.

9.0 a.m. Your job—whatever it may be, school or otherwise.

1.0 p.m. Lunch—not too heavy.

2.0 p.m. Work—or cricket, if you are lucky.

4.30 p.m. Tea and rest.

5.0 p.m. Cricket, if you are still lucky, or practice.

NOTE: Get some fielding practice or a field out, if you can.

6.30 p.m. Change and a shower.

7.0 p.m. Main meal—but take it slowly.

8.0 p.m. Read, mainly cricket books. Or homework.

9.0 p.m. Bed.

REMEMBER: It is along Regularity Road that you must go if you want to get to the beautiful City of Health. And good health is essential to a Cricketer.

NOTE: Always be clean, inside and outside. A dirty body means that the sweat pores are closed up, and the acids inside you cannot come out.

REMEMBER: "A sweat a day keeps the doctor away" more than any old apple ever did.

One need not tell a fellow like you to be clean inside. A Cricketer always is. Do not forget the old proverb: "It is not Cricket." That applies to many things.

All these things that I have told you should be easy to anyone who is really keen on being a real Cricketer.

Now let us see about some of the phrases that Cricketers use.

NINTH WICKET

Cricket Vocabulary, etc.

Ashes. When Australia beat England for the first time, a newspaper published an "Epitaph" on English cricket which "died at the Oval. The body will be cremated and the ashes taken to Australia." Later some English ladies had an urn made containing the ashes of a bat. This is the origin of the Ashes.

Averages. The number of runs scored by a batsman divided by the number of times he has been out. Should be big. Or the number of runs scored off a bowler, in hits only, divided by the number of wickets he takes. Should be small. In any case, do not think of averages while you are playing.

Bail. The two pieces of wood on top of the stumps. If either bail is moved out of position you are out, even if it does not fall to the ground.

Ball. A full-sized ball weighs $5\frac{1}{2}$ to $5\frac{3}{4}$ ounces. The smaller, for chaps under fourteen, weighs an ounce less.

Blob. (See Duck.)

Body Line. An attack by short-pitched balls on the batsman's body. (See Leg Theory.)

BOSIE. (See GOOGLIE.)

BREAK. A ball that changes direction from Off or Leg when it pitches.

BYE. When the ball is untouched by the batsman, and passes the wicket-keeper, the batsman can run. These are called Byes. If the ball goes to boundary, it counts as four Byes.

CATCH. To make a Catch, you must hold the ball off the ground for three seconds. *But* if you use your cap or any other part of your clothes, it counts five runs to the other side, as well as being not out.

CENTRE. (See MIDDLE.)

CENTURY. A hundred runs scored by a batsman in one innings. Hobbs holds the record with 197 centuries in first-class cricket. W. G. Grace made the first "Century of Centuries."

COVER POINT. Fields on the off, between Point and Mid-off. He should note that most balls come to him with a left-hand swerve.

CUT. A stroke played by coming well across to a short ball on the Off, and placing it, with a more or less horizontal bat, between Point and the Slips.

CUT DRIVE. This stroke is played with the bat at an angle of about 60° at a half-volley.

DRIVE. A forward stroke caught on the half-volley and sent, preferably along the carpet, anywhere between Cover and Mid-wicket.

RIGHT
"No words needed"

Duck. No runs in an innings—from the shape of the big round O on the score-board, which is like a duck's egg.

Extras. Byes, Wides, Leg-byes or No-balls. If any of these go to the boundary they count as four—called Sundries in Australia.

Forward. A batsman should play forward to a ball when he can reach where it pitches.

Field. All the space inside the boundary. In the ideal field the boundary should be seventy to eighty yards from either wicket.

Boundary. The outside limit of the field. A ball travelling over the boundary counts four runs. If the batsman hits the ball over the boundary without its touching the ground, it usually counts six runs.

  Note: If a fieldsman, in stopping a ball, has any part of himself on the ground and over the boundary, it is four runs. Similarly, if a fieldsman, in trying to catch a ball, steps over the boundary, it counts as a six, and the batsman is *not out*.

Glide. A fine shot to Leg, played with a straight bat, and edged past Long Leg. Takes a good deal of judging and practice.

Glove. The "Fit On" Batting Glove, especially if it is open at the palm, is more comfortable than the "wrap-round-the-thumb" sort. In either case, do not wear them too tight.

WRONG
"No words needed"

- **Googlie.** An Off-break with a Leg-break action, or, more difficult, a Leg-break with an Off-break action. No good without a perfect length. Invented by B. J. T. Bosanquet. That is why it is called a "Bosie" in Australia.

- **Guard.** Before you start your innings, you ask the umpire for Guard. Usually your bat should cover the middle stump. If you are inclined to stand very near your bat it may be as well to take middle-and-leg, or even, in extreme cases, leg stump. This is a more or less safe guard against Leg before Wicket. (Sometimes called "Covering one" or "One leg.") Please hold your bat up straight when taking guard. It helps the umpire a lot. Do not make too big a "block." Just a scratch on the ground with a bail should be enough.

- **Hat Trick.** Three wickets taken, i.e., caught, bowled or stumped, or leg before wicket, off a bowler with successive balls. The end of an over does not break a hat-trick so long as the balls are bowled consecutively. You will receive a brand-new hat for performing this feat—if you are lucky!

- **Hook.** A short ball to Leg can be "Hooked" over the left shoulder in the direction of Square-leg. You want a good eye to do this shot, because, if you miss it, it may get you instead.

- **Innings.** Lasts until a batsman, or the whole side, is out.

FORWARD DEFENCE

NOTE.—Well pitched-up, but on the wicket. Left elbow and wrist well forward

Leg. The whole field to the left, if you are right-handed, or to the right, if you are left-handed, of a line drawn through the middle stumps.

L.B.W. If the ball pitches on the wicket, and you stop it with any part of your person—even your head—and it would have hit the wicket, you are out "Leg before Wicket." By the new rule you are out if the ball pitches outside the off-stump and breaks in to the wicket. Always—

Remember the umpire knows best, and, apart from the bowler, is the only person on the field who possibly can know, and the bowler not always. If he gives you out, do not grouse about it. You have got your marching orders, and that's that.

Leg Theory. An attack, by bowling shortish on the Leg side. There is a group of fieldsmen to Leg, corresponding to slips. The idea is to make the ball swing away so that one of these fellows may snap up a mis-hit. It is rather unavoidable that a ball or two gets near the batsman, and "body line" results.

M.C.C. The Marylebone Cricket Club, with its headquarters at Lord's, is the Parliament of Cricket. It makes all the Laws of the Game.

Middle. (Sometimes called Centre.) The Guard covering the middle stump.

Middle and Leg. The Guard covering the space between the middle and leg stumps. (Sometimes called "Covering both" or "Two leg.")

[*Keystone View Company*]

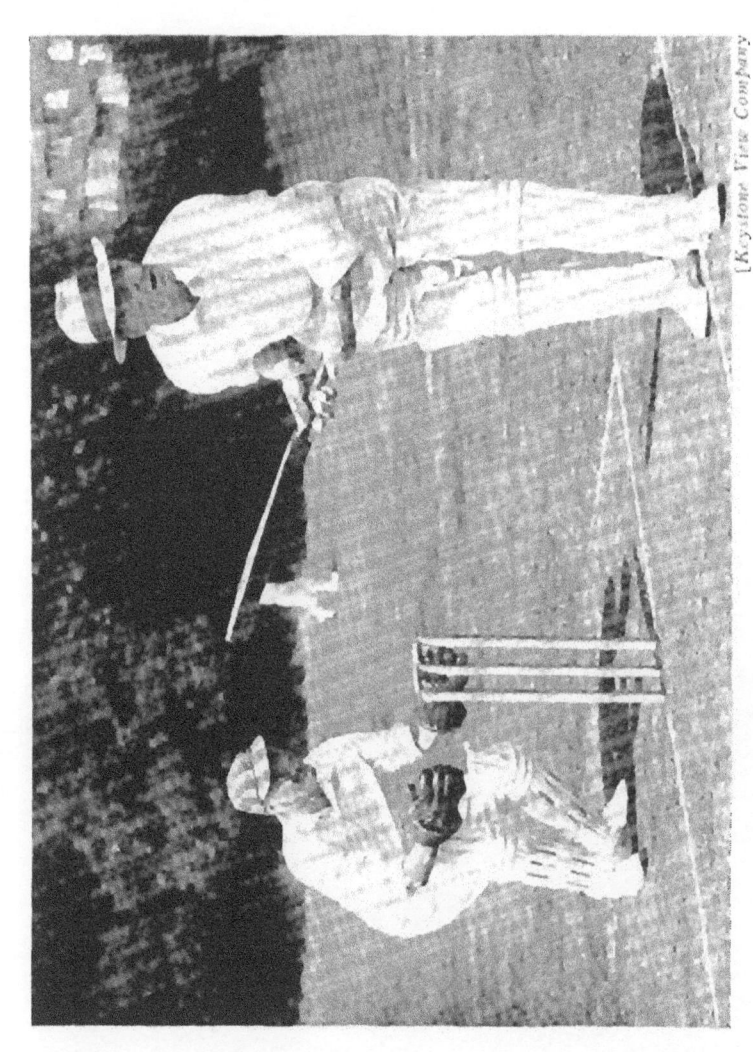

Do you remember "The Lives of a Bengal Lancer"?
Here's AUBREY SMITH batting

HAMMOND'S OFF-DRIVE

NOTE.—His head was right over where his bat connected with the ball

Not Out. One batsman on a side is bound to be Not Out. This helps his average—not that that matters.

No Ball. The bowler is allowed one foot over the bowling crease. If the other foot so much as touches that crease, it is a No Ball, and the batsman can do what he likes with it. Also, if the bowler's arm is bent when he delivers the ball, it is a No Ball. The only way a batsman can be out to a No Ball is by being run out.

Off. The half of the field in front of the batsman, bounded by a line drawn through the stumps.

Off Theory. An attack by the bowler bowling on, or just outside the off-stump, and swinging away. The eager, grasping hands of the Slips are waiting for it.

Out. Bowled (which includes played on from the bat or any part of the batsman's person)—caught—stumped—leg before wicket—all count to the bowler. Run out does not.

Over. Used to be four balls bowled from each end alternatively. It was increased to five, and then six. In Australia it is now eight balls.

Over-throws. If a fieldsman throws in the ball, and it is missed, you can run, and every run is added to whatever score you have already made.

Note: You are not allowed to run over-throws from the wicket-keeper's return to the bowler.

Pad. Take care that the straps of your pads are well tucked in.

Note: Pads should be strapped with buckles outside.

Run. To complete a run, the batsman must cross and make good his ground, i.e., either the bat or some part of the batsman must be *on* the ground *over* the crease; the other one goes back to where he started from if the two batsmen have not crossed and one of them is caught.

Note: You should never run up the middle of the pitch. The striker runs up and down towards the side the bowler has bowled from. The non-striker runs up and down his own side.

Remember: The non-striker should always back up from the moment the bowler has bowled.

Also Note: Always run the first run hard. There may be a second.

Run Out. Slide your bat along edgewise on the ground well in front of you.

Note: *On* the crease counts as out or a Short Run.

Remember: If the wicket is already broken, the fieldsman must hold the ball in one hand and pull a stump out of the ground with the other to run a batsman out.

Scorer. The fellow who keeps the score-book nice and tidy. He must always answer the umpire's signals by raising his hand.

"FINISH OF AN ON-DRIVE"
NOTE.—It went between mid-on and mid-wicket

Short. Any ball bowled so far up the pitch that the batsman cannot reach it is Short.

Short Run. If you do not complete a run properly (see Run above), the umpire will yell out "One Short," perhaps "Two Short," etc., and it will not count.

Signals. The umpire uses the following signals: (a) for a Bye he holds one hand up; (b) for a Leg-bye he lifts one foot and slaps his leg; (c) for Out he lifts one arm with the forefinger up; (d) for a Wide he extends both arms outwards; (e) for Not Out he shakes his head; (f) for a boundary hit for four he waves one hand from side to side; (g) for a six he holds both hands above his head; (h) for a boundary Bye he lifts one hand and waves the other from side to side; (i) for a No Ball he lifts one hand and yells: "No Ball" as quickly as he can.

Slip. The one, two or three gentlemen who stand, with grasping hands, behind the wicket-keeper on the Off, waiting for that snick off the edge of the bat.

Stumped. If neither the batsman, nor his bat, is on the ground *over* the crease, the wicket-keeper can put the wicket down, and that batsman has to go.

Note: If any part of the wicket-keeper is in front of the wicket when he puts it down, it counts as Not Out. Also—

NOTE: The wicket-keeper must have the ball *in* his hand when he puts the wicket down, and the ball itself must touch the stumps.

SUBSTITUTE. If one of your side is unable to carry on, you may bring in a Substitute, but he is only allowed to field. He must not bat, nor bowl, nor even keep wicket.

THROW. The bowler's arm must be straight when he delivers a ball, otherwise it is a NO BALL.

THROW IN. Always throw in overhand. From a long distance the ball should pitch short enough to reach the wicket at the height of the bails. This makes it easy to put the wicket down. From a short distance you can throw in full pitch.

NOTE: Throwing in cannot be practised enough.

UMPIRE. There are two Umpires—one behind the bowler's wicket, who judges Caught Wicket and Leg before Wicket chiefly, and one at Square Leg, who judges Stumped chiefly, and Run Out.

WICKET. The wickets should be 22 yards apart. In under-fourteen-year-old games it is usually 21 yards.

WIDE. If a ball is bowled so that it is out of the batsman's reach in any direction, it is a Wide. If it goes to the boundary it counts as four wides.

BUMP BALL. If the ball strikes the ground and bat at the same time and rises, it may seem like a catch—but it is not: it is a bump ball.

YORKER. A ball that pitches pretty well on the batsman's crease. It is a beast. You cannot get it on the half-volley or full toss. Just bring your bat straight down on top of it, and thank your lucky stars if you keep it out of your wicket.

Just a few flashes about some Cricket Personalities. This, of course, cannot be a complete list. A whole book would not be enough for that. They are just "picked out of the hat."

Let's take them in two lots—the real "Old Timers," whose ghosts haunt Hambledon and Lord's—the "Old Brigade" whose Test Match days are over, though some are carrying on in the less strenuous atmosphere of county cricket.

REAL OLD TIMERS

(The dates in brackets are the years in which they were born.)

Bannerman, Chas. (1851) made the first century—152 not out—in Test Match history. Australian.

Bedham, W. (1766), the finest bat of his day. Called Silver Billy. Played for Hambledon. Died aged 96, so nearly "made a century."

NINTH WICKET

Beauclerk, Lord Frederick (?), a great personality. One of the first of the "Sporting Parsons." But he was sometimes suspected of betting and sharpish practices.

Bligh, The Hon. Ivo (later Earl of Darnley) (1859), was named "Saint" Ivo, when he led a "pilgrimage" to Australia to get back the Ashes.

Brearley, Walter (1876), Lancashire amateur fast bowler. Great athlete, and cheery, expert leg-puller. Always jumped the pavilion rails.

Cæsar, Julius (1830)—note the name—Surrey professional.

Caffyn, William (1828), played for Surrey and New South Wales!

Lillywhite, James (1825), Great Sussex bowler. Initiated *The Cricketer's Guide*, a predecessor of *Wisden's Almanac*.

Marlborough, Duke of (?), soldier and cricketer—a great combination!

Mynn, Alfred (1807), a whole book could be written about him. He was magnificently built—a huge man. Like all really *big* men, was as gentle as a lamb. He was the best batsman of his time, and no mean bowler. Upright and honest, he was an example to all men, on and off the field. His charities covered a wide area, and he died mourned by many.

Pilch, Fuller (1803), came near to Alfred Mynn as a cricketer. Both played for Kent.

Small, Tom (?), all-rounder, bat-maker, fiddler, full of wit.

Stevens, Lumpy (?), the great bowler of his day. Both these lived about a century ago.

    NOTE: How the South predominated at first. Kent, Sussex, Surrey became the "cradle" of the game, with headquarters at Broadhalfpenny Down, Hambledon.

THE OLD BRIGADE

Abel, Bobby (1857), called the "Guvnor." Diminutive, bespectacled later, but with astonishing power. Top score 357 at the Oval.

Armstrong, W. W. (1879), huge, batsman, slow bowler. Australia's captain after the War—one of the best captains of all time.

Bardsley, W. (1883), Australian, brilliant left-hander. First to score two centuries in a Test Match.

Barnes, S. F. (1873), the "Compleat Bowler." Medium, mixed them, ran through powerful Australian teams on perfect wickets, helped by F. R. Foster (fast left-hand). Played many years for Staffordshire (Minor County).

Blythe, Colin (1879), Kentish slow left-hand bowler. A delightful personality. Musician. Killed in the War.

Bosanquet, B. J. T. (1877), originally a fast bowler, invented the "Googlie" and astonished the Aussies.

Carr, D. W. (1872), schoolmaster. Took up googlie bowling late in cricket life (nearly forty) and suddenly became good enough for England. "It's never too late——"

Cameron, H. B. (1905), South Africa's finest wicket-keeper. A good bat. Unhappily, he died, aged thirty.

Challenor, George (1888), the Hobbs of the West Indies. A magnificent bat.

Chapman, A. P. F. (1900), big, cheery personality. Brilliant left-hand hitter and marvellous field. Regained the Ashes in his first match as captain of England (Oval, 1926).

Chester, F. (1894) played for Worcester as a boy of seventeen. Made many centuries in brilliant style. Most promising all-rounder for years. Lost an arm. Is now one of the keenest, and best, umpires in the world.

Douglas, J. W. H. T. (1882), a grand man, champion boxer, captain of England and winner of the Ashes, untiring fast bowler full of endeavour, slow, determined batsman (Australians nicknamed him "Johnny-Won't-Hit-To-Day"). Died in vain attempt to save his father's life in a shipwreck.

Ferris, J. J. (1867), Australian bowler. See Turner.

Fry, C. B. (1872), Wonderful all-round athlete. Held long-jump and high-jump records. Blues for cricket, soccer, athletics, and, nearly, rugger. Made stacks of runs for Sussex.

Gilligan, A. E. R. (1894), Dulwich College, Surrey, Sussex and England. No captain after the War got nearer to winning the Ashes in Australia.

Grace, W. G. (1848), County Cap at sixteen. "W.G.," "The Doctor," "The Old Man." Swept like a flame over the Cricket World. Weighed nearly 20 stone before he gave up first-class cricket. See "Tenth Wicket."

Harris, Lord (1851), Kent and England. President of the M.C.C. A great batsman and personality.

Hawke, Lord (1860), captain of England and Yorkshire. Known in the West Indies as "de Lawd."

Hayward, Tom (1872), Hobbs's predecessor. They put on a hundred for the first wicket for Surrey many times.

Headley, George (1909), the "Black Bradman." Makes phenomenal scores for the West Indies.

Hendren, "Patsy" (Elias) (1884), one of the great personalities of the game. Has helped England out of many a tight corner. Always cheery. Has a special little corner of his own in the changing-room at Lord's which he considers lucky. A wonderful fielder.

Hill, Clem (1877), the Australian left-handed "Ninety King." Has scored more "nervous nineties" in Test Matches than any other player.

Hirst, George (1871), jovial, Yorkshire left-hand fast-medium bowler and useful batsman. A real fighter and a splendid coach.

Hobbs, J. B. (1882), for many years the world's best batsman. The best type of cricketer. As popular in Australia and South Africa as in his own country. Holds the record for the greatest number of centuries—197. As he lost the War years and one season later, when he was ill, there is no knowing how far he would have gone.

Jackson, F. S. (now Sir Stanley Jackson) (1870), famous all-rounder. Won toss in all five Test Matches here. Never had the time to visit Australia.

Jessop, G. L. ("The Croucher") (1874), with a magnificent eye and powerful shoulders reduced "slogging" to a science. Made one glorious century enabling England to beat Australia. A splendid fieldsman and fast bowler.

Larwood, Harold (1904), has now given up Test cricket. The most accurate fast bowler of modern times. Perfected "Leg Theory." Made 98 in a Test and several centuries in County cricket.

Lilley, A. A. (Dick) (1867), England's wicket-keeper for years. A reliable bat.

Macartney, C. G. (1886), a daring batsman, whose footwork was marvellous. Made a century before lunch for Australia v. England. Called the "Governor-General."

MacGregor, Gregor (1869), England wicket-keeper. Stood up to faster bowling. Played rugger for Scotland.

MacLaren, A. C. (1873), great batsman. Captained England for many years.

Noble, M. A. (1873), one of the greatest Australian captains. All-rounder.

Ponsford, W. H. (1900), hero of several long-stand records against, together with Bradman. Only batsman to make over 400 twice in first-class cricket.

Ranjitsinhji, K. S. (H.H. the Jam Sahib of Nawanagar) (1872), known affectionately to the British public as "Ranji." The most graceful batsman of late years. His leg glides off fast bowling were miraculous. A splendid field and no mean bowler.

Rhodes, Wilfred (1877), typical Yorkshire cricketer. Started as purely a left-hand, extraordinarily accurate, slow bowler, breaking the ball either way. Developed his batting so well that he holds Test record, with Hobbs, of 323 for the first wicket. Only one to have been recognized first and last wicket man for England.

Richardson, Tom (1870), burly, lion-hearted Surrey and England fast bowler. Could bowl all day without bowling a single loose ball. Came from Mitcham—a great cricket centre.

Scotton, W. (1853), reliable bat—but painfully slow. Held record for many years by batting against Australia for 67 minutes without scoring. Once made 7 while W. G. Grace made 100.

Smith, C. A. (1863), slow bowler. "Round the corner Smith," so called owing to his curious curving run up to the wicket. Played against South Africa. Now Aubrey Smith, famous film star. Has made great progress with cricket in Hollywood.

Spofforth, F. R. (1853), "The Demon." Very tall, dark and fierce-looking, fast bowler. Took a terrifying spring as he bowled—and many English wickets. Left Australia and settled here. Practised every day, summer and winter.

Sutcliffe, H. (1894), after Hobbs retired became England's No. 1 "Rock of Gibraltar." Dour Yorkshire fighter. Has spent many hours at the wicket defying Australia's bowling might.

Tate, M. W. (1895), great-hearted fast-medium bowler and dangerous hitter. Noted for huge feet and vast shoulders and a smile like dawn over the desert. Holds record for number of wickets in one series of Tests—38. Changes pace and makes the ball do weird things.

Taylor, H. W. (1889), the "Hobbs" of South Africa.

Turner, C. T. B. (1862), with J. J. Ferris formidable bowling partnership for Australia. Swept England like a typhoon—"Turner the Terror" and "Ferris the Fiend."

Trumper, Victor (1877), brilliant Australian No. 1. For many years held Test record for number of centuries.

Warner, P. F. (1873), "Plum" to the cricket world. Captain of England and Middlesex. Has made runs in practically every cricket-playing country on the globe. Has more to do with directing the destinies of Cricket nowadays than any other man. Editor of *The Cricketer*.

Woolley, F. E. (1887), model left-hander. Perfect timing makes him appear to hit with little effort—but the ball travels, as Kent's opponents will tell you. Once made two 90's in a Test *v.* Australia. Brilliant slip fieldsman. Used to be a fine left-hand slow bowler.

Woods, S. M. J. (1868), great, burly Australian. Played cricket for Australia and rugger for England. Fast bowler, hard-hitting batsman.

"England's hopes," such as W. R. Hammond, are still "working out their destinies."

HERE ARE A FEW ODDS AND ENDS:

Cricket often runs in families. Well-known families are the Ashtons, Bryans, Days and Gunns. Australia has the Gregory family. Then the Gilligan family made their bow. Now comes that marvellous family of Graces. W. G., E. M., E. F. all played for England. The rest were cricketers of no inconsiderable skill. By the way, the mother, Mrs. H. M. Grace, is the only woman mentioned in *Wisden's*.

The Hearnes of Kent did yeoman service. The Steels and the Studds, from North and South respectively, make their mark. Sir J. E. K. Studd became Lord Mayor of London.

The Tyldesleys, two separate families, have been mainstays of Lancashire for generations.

The Walkers of Southgate became a byword in Club cricket.

Finally, the Lyttelton family, besides inscribing their names on Cricket's roll of fame, have done more than their bit for the Empire.

Three sets of twins have played in first-class cricket in England. The Dentons of Northamptonshire, the Rippons of Somersetshire, the Stephens of Warwickshire. More than once scorers have asked them to wear some distinguishing mark!

Cases of fathers and sons are rare. Tate, Fred, missed a vital catch in a Test. He was properly "ticked off," and told that no member of his family would ever play for England again. Yet Maurice Tate, his son, became England's "stock bowler." M. R. Jardine was a first-class cricketer and a Blue.

His son, D. R. Jardine, went further still. He captained England in Australia and won the Ashes.

A last note. All the three Indians who have played for England made centuries in their first Test Matches against Australia. "Ranji" made 175 at Sydney. And he had risen from his sick-bed, suffering from pleurisy, to do so. K. S. Duleepsinhji ("Ranji's" nephew) made 173 at Lord's, and the Nawab of Pataudi made 102 at Sydney.

I could tell you lots more, but the "Tenth Wicket" calls!

TENTH WICKET

A Few Yarns

TAKE a journey through England in May.

In the towns the youngsters are playing the old Game with an apology for a ball, a bit of rough-hewn wood for a bat, and a lamp-post or a petrol-tin for a wicket.

Some will be playing with tennis-ball and stump against a wicket marked in chalk on the wall of their asphalt playground.

The public parks claim many. And here the Game takes a bit more shape. There are stumps, old club bats and balls, and organized matches.

Others are luckier, in spotless flannels, with expensive gear and on perfect wickets, at their public schools.

Yet the same spirit animates them all—to whack that ball into the next parish, to spreadeagle that chap's wickets with a hot 'un, or to catch him out.

Cricket at school! What memories! The Old Boy, thinking back, conjures up visions of summer days. And summer days mean cricket.

A certain school has a Good-bye Song, sung by those who are leaving. One verse runs:

> Oh, those pleasant days on the level grass
> 'Neath a glorious summer sky,
> When the ball on the bat sweet music made
> 'Mid the mingled cries of "Well bowled! Well played!"
> Till the trees stretched far their evening shade——
> But now we must say "Good-bye."

At school one graduates from the "out-of-course-and-it's-my-knock-now" days to the more lordly atmosphere of the Eleven.

Just an incident that happened. Playing in a small game, I happened to hit a ball right through the Second Eleven match (our ground had a very park-like look on half-holidays when there was no First Eleven school match). The aristocrats of the Second Eleven would not let our fieldsman through, so he had to go round. Moreover, the ball had to be thrown back *round* the match. By the time its Odyssey was over, we had run ten! As this gave me my fifty and the last man was in, I was mightily pleased!

After school-days, some go to Club cricket, some are lost to the game through claims of occupation or duty, and some retire to the country and fatten on village cricket. The genii get their Blues and travel on to first-class cricket, and a happy few play for England.

Nearly all teams, happily, include an humorist. In Test matches, though, and it is a thing one sneakingly regrets, the game is played with such deadly seriousness that humour is rather frowned upon. One cannot imagine W. G. Grace's experience in Australia happening now, for instance. Jones, the Australian fast bowler, bowled a shortish ball which got up and bisected W. G.'s big black beard. In terrible indignation, the Old Man yelled down the pitch: "What the blazes are you playing at, Jonah?" Jones meekly, but, one suspects, with his tongue in his cheek, replied: "Sorry, Doctor, she slipped!"

Tom Emmett, the old Yorkshire bowler, was a great comedian. On one occasion he was bowling to the greatest batsman of his time. After being knocked about unmercifully, although he was bowling well, he said loudly, with an humorous air of resignation: "Ah poots 'em wheer Ah likes, but 'e," pointing with his thumb, "poots 'em wheer 'e likes."

Johnny Briggs, who was taken ill during a Test Match and died later, was a real, irrepressible Lancashire "Lad."

Nowadays, we have the bubbling effervescence of George Duckworth, and the vast, infectious grin of Maurice Tate.

Many cricketers have quaint mannerisms. Not exactly superstitions, but queer little customs.

"Plum" Warner always would wear a faded old Harlequin cap, which became well known in practically every cricket-loving country in the world. And his sailor-like hitch of his "slacks" with his right hand, before getting ready to take the bowling, became a national institution.

By the way, "Plum" is the only cricketer ever to have had his photograph twice in *Wisden's Almanac* among the "Five Cricketers of the Year" series.

I shall never forget the scene at Lord's in 1921 when Middlesex won the Championship by beating Surrey in a grand race against time. It was "Plum's" last match. I had just landed back from a visit to Berlin early that morning. But I went straight to Lord's, and had my reward in seeing one of the finest day's cricket it was possible to see. Twenty-five thousand people rushed the ground at the end. "Plum" was chaired to the pavilion and had to make a speech. It was an unforgettable sight.

Tom Hayward, the first batsman after W. G. Grace to score a hundred centuries, used to push the peak of his cap farther back the longer he batted, exposing a vast expanse of forehead. Whenever he approached the second hundred, his cap was nearly falling off the back of his head. If he ever made three hundred, he must have wanted a piece of elastic!

Jack Hobbs is supposed always to have put his left pad and glove on first. He also had a habit of lifting his bat up with both hands and shrugging his shoulders, as though his shirt didn't fit. He then used to twirl his bat round in his left hand once or twice before settling down to his stance.

A memorable, and unforgettable, scene was enacted at the Oval on the occasion of Hobbs's last appearance against Australia. He came in as usual, and the whole Australian team gathered in a circle round him and gave him three cheers—a signal honour to a gallant "friend the enemy."

Cricket does not seem to produce the personalities nowadays.

Once, when W. G. made a century at Lord's, some tame statistician counted the number of balls that passed his bat. During the making of those hundred runs there were only four balls with which W. G.'s bat failed to connect. Shades of off and leg theories! What would W. G. have done with the off theory and the leg ditto? One rather suspects that, with his enormous height, he would have found a way of clouting both those insidious demons out of existence.

Scotton was W. G.'s first-wicket partner on several occasions. He was painfully slow, but very sure. He once stayed in for sixty-seven minutes in a Test Match without scoring! This record was, I believe, beaten later by D. R. Jardine. *Punch's* opinion of Scotton was once expressed thus:

> Block, block, block,
> At the foot of thy wicket, O Scotton!
> I would that my tongue could utter
> My boredom.
> You won't put the "pot on!"
>
> .   .   .   .   .
>
> One hour of Grace or Walter Read
> Were worth a week of you.

(Walter Read, by the way, once went in at No. 10 for England and made a century.)

Joe Darling, Australian captain, was not as bad as Scotton, but he was a steady bat and made many big scores. After one of his long innings, it was written:

> In the timber-yard, my Darling,
>   When the ball is trundled low,
> And the fieldsmen, vainly snarling,
>   Quickly come and quickly go——
> And the bowling, getting brisker,
>   Giving you but strength anew,
> Makes the long-stop gnash his whisker,
>   And the cover-point look blue.

Yes, one does sneakingly regret those days.

Even county cricket is not so full of yarns as it used to be, but there are signs that the old, light-hearted days are returning.

A certain county cricketer was *never* out leg before wicket. It was just impossible! Yet it happened. One dread day the umpire raised his finger and out our friend had to go. At close of play, he tackled the umpire in the dressing-room and explained exactly how he could not have been out. The umpire, a true North-countryman, made reply: "Eh, lad, tha wastna aout? Well, joost tha loook in t' papers termorrer!"

W. G. was a supreme leg-puller. But it was extremely difficult to elongate his limb. There is a story about him, true or not. As captain of Gloucester, he was a regular martinet, and always insisted on his team, when on tour, being in bed by 10 p.m. He himself could stay up all night! Two Cambridge undergraduates, who were playing for the county in an away match, thought they would catch the Old Man out. So, one night, they set the old water-jug trap over his hotel room door and retired round an angle of the corridor to await events. At about midnight, W. G. came lumbering down the passage. He gave one glance at his door, kicked it open from the outside so that the jug fell harmlessly inside, walked straight round the corner and knocked the heads of those two bright lads together. W. G. is credited with the longest drive ever made. Playing on a London Club ground which skirted the railway, he hit a ball into the window of a passing express, which did not stop till it reached Dover—a distance of seventy-two miles! Some drive!

G. L. Jessop, the greatest and most scientific slogger of all time, toured with an M.C.C. team to the United States and Canada. The American papers described him as "the human catapult, who wrecks the roofs of distant towns when set in his assault!"

When batting in Canada, on a ground whose boundary was the forty-ninth parallel of latitude, the frontier between Canada and the United States of America, Jessop is said to have hit a ball "from the British Empire to America!"

Many a good story is told of E. M. Grace, W. G.'s little brother, who was a pocket edition, complete with beard and all, of the Old Man. He never could take his cricket too seriously. When he was captain of his local side, he and another batsman were having a regular tussle as to which of them would head the batting averages at the end of the season. The last match came, and they were about equal. They opened the innings together, and the other fellow made about fifty and got out. E. M. had also made fifty. Next ball he skied very high towards cover, who was a safe catch. With the ball still in the air, and a broad smile on his face, E. M. shouted: "I declare the innings closed!" So he headed the averages by virtue of the not out! In another match the irrepressible E. M. was batting at the opposite end to the pavilion. A loud appeal for leg before wicket went up. The umpire raised his hand. E. M., looking slightly surprised, went. When he got to the pavilion, he was told that he was not out. The umpire had merely raised his finger to deal with an errant fly which had alighted on his nose. The fieldsmen had, of course, kept mum, scenting a rag. E. M. knew perfectly well that, if he went back, he would be in front of his crease, and that the wicket-keeper would put the wicket down and claim a "run out." So, taking his bat between his teeth, he crawled round on hands and knees behind the line of spectators until he was behind the batting crease, then, strutting jauntily on to the field, he continued his innings.

One of the very greatest charms of cricket is that it is a game for everybody—prince or peasant, duke or dustman. It is equally enjoyed by all together.

In about 1750, Frederick, the then Prince of Wales, was very fond of the game. Unfortunately, he did not enjoy the best of health, and actually died partly from the effect of a blow from a cricket ball.

King Edward VII was a very keen cricketer and had a private ground in Windsor Park. His cousin, Prince Christian Victor, was a brilliant batsman, who would have made his mark in county cricket if he could have spared the time from his military duties. He once made a double century in India. This stood as the record for many years for the highest score made in Indian cricket. The Prince died fighting for his country in Africa.

The history of cricket, ancient and modern, is studded with titles.

Before the days of county cricket, noblemen used to run their own teams, and back them for large sums of money against the teams of other noblemen. The Duke of Marlborough, the great General, was exceptionally keen. He got into serious trouble once for playing in a match on a Sunday!

Probably these matches were the forerunners of county cricket.

In modern times, our aristocracy has played its part in cricket.

Lord Hawke captained England and Yorkshire, and was the finest batsman in the "county of broad acres." Lord Tennyson played one of the pluckiest fighting innings ever played for England. His right hand was broken and practically useless. The Australian bowlers included J. M. Gregory and Macdonald, the greatest fast "shock" attack Australia ever had. Yet Lord Tennyson, to all intents and purposes one-handed, made sixty-three extremely valuable runs. Lord Aberdare, as the Hon. C. N. Bruce, flicked many a boundary past cover for Middlesex with iron wrists made hard and supple by racquets.

There are many others, but this little list will suffice.

English village cricket is a delightful world of its own. It is full of keenness and humour. I must tell you a couple of personal, true-to-life yarns. I was playing in an inter-village match in the West-country. Each side, for obvious reasons, had its own umpire. I was bowling at our umpire's end, and bowled a ball that might, or might not, have pitched on the leg stump. At any rate, it came in

K

a bit. The batsman missed it and it hit his pad. I did not feel like appealing, but, before I could even think of doing so, our priceless umpire, with both hands raised well above his head, yelled: "Aow's that? Aout!"

The village we played in our "local Derby" had a fast bowler. Larwood may be *a* fast bowler, but this was *the* fast bowler. He hardly had Larwood's control of length, though! Batting against him was rather like being under shell-fire. On our ground there was a very short boundary behind mid-on. The speedster dished me up a beautiful half-volley first ball. More by good luck than by judgment, my bat connected. The ball cleared mid-on's head and just plomped over the short boundary for six. The bowler gave me one look. He then removed his waistcoat, which he neatly folded and handed to the umpire. Retiring to the end of his run, which he lengthened to about thirty yards, he carefully placed his cloth cap on the ground. He gave me another good long look and then charged towards the crease like an enraged bull. A whirl of arms, and the next thing I knew was my off stump cavorting towards first slip, the wicket-keeper neatly fielding the middle stump, and the bails disappearing into the middle distance! I never even saw that ball!

Cricket in India is a joy. Soldiers make good cricketers and vice versa. Besides, the wonderfully clear atmosphere gives one a clear sight of the ball. As grass is often conspicuous by its absence, matting frequently has to be used.

An incident, nearly forgotten, comes to mind. It was at Rawalpindi, in a Regimental match—Royal Artillery *v.* Royal Corps of Signals, if I remember aright. A certain Bombardier carried his bat right through the Artillery innings. When the last wicket fell, he was alas! 98 not out. And he had never made a century. He happened to overhear someone whisper to the scorer: "Couldn't you re-count and add a couple to ———'s score?" The Bombardier was furious, and it nearly ended in a fight. That was the spirit! He wasn't going to take what he hadn't earned fairly.

About the same time a new draft came out from England in charge of a young officer. This lad was rather shy and retiring. The men couldn't quite make him out, so they didn't take to him much. But his chance came. He was asked to play against another Battery for the Brigade Cup. Going in fifth wicket down, after a collapse, he absolutely collared the bowling and scored a brilliant century on a wicket that was not too true. Thereby his batting won the game. From that moment the men loved him, and he became one of the most popular officers in the Brigade. This drew him out of his shell and increased his efficiency as an officer by hundreds per cent.

I was once bowling against a team of Sikhs. A new batsman came in. First he took "centre" guard, and carefully scratched a line from the block-hole to the middle stump with a bail. Then he started all over again and took "leg stump" guard. Once more he removed a bail and drew another line from block to leg stump. Carefully placing his feet so that the toes were "toeing the line" on the leg stump line (to prevent l.b.w., I suppose), he took "middle and leg" guard. The poor bowler meanwhile was fuming. When Old Finicky at last was ready, the bowler took his run. The first ball was a slowish full toss on the base of the off stump. A wild swing—a complete miss—and the off peg lying flat!

To return home, here is a curious, but perfectly true, incident. A schoolboy bowler had some remarkable feats to his credit during term-time. He was asked to play in a club trial match in the holidays. On being put on to bowl, he sweetly asked his captain: "Shall I bowl right-hand or left?" Collapse of captain. Apparently the lad was ambidextrous, and bowled fastish left or slow right!

If you were asked what was the highest score made by any batsman in a single innings, could you answer? As a matter of fact, it is 628 not out, made by A. E. J. Collins in a house match at Clifton College. His knock lasted for five afternoons. So he had to play himself in again four times. A pretty useful show. Bradman, of course, holds the record for the highest score in first-class cricket. He made 452 not out for New South Wales against Queensland. W. H. Ponsford is the only batsman to make over 400 twice, both in State matches in Australia. In England, A. C. MacLaren made 424 for Lancashire *v.* Somerset at Taunton. Over a thousand has been made by a side in a single innings twice by Victoria. The scoreboard must have looked funny!

The Hon. F. S. (now Sir Stanley) Jackson, when captain of England, won the toss in all five Tests against Australia—the only time it has happened. England won with a good deal to spare.

One often hears of a bowler "dishing up a wide long hop" to a batsman who is near his century. Or a fieldsman deliberately missing a catch in the same circumstances. Personally, I don't believe in that sort of thing. In the first place, if a batsman makes a mistake, he should pay for it, whether he is nearing a hundred or not. Secondly, it really can't give him much satisfaction to have a century "presented" to him like that. He knows, in his own heart, that he hasn't really deserved it.

I was fielding on the boundary in a house match at school once. "A. Dash" had made 97—the nearest approach he had ever got, to date, to making the coveted hundred. He skied one towards me, nearly a six, but not quite. For a wonder, I judged it well and got right underneath it. Two thoughts were in my mind while that ball was dropping: "How I should like to drop it and give Dash his chance for a century," and: "This is a close match and every run counts." Anyway, second thoughts won. I held the catch and Dash had to go.

Talking of nineties, did you know that Clem Hill, the left-hander, made 99, 98, 97, 96 in consecutive innings for Australia in Test Matches? Later he made a 90! The "nervous nineties" with a vengeance!

The hardest luck of all came the way of Chipperfield, of Australia. In his very first Test Match he played a magnificent fighting innings when his side was collapsing. He was 99 not out at the luncheon interval. During the interval he grew "nervouser and nervouser." He wasn't helped by people crowding round him and giving him advice. Result: he played all round the first ball after lunch, and went—still 99! Still, he has the consolation of having broken a record—the first man to make 99 in his first Test.

Woolley also made 96 and 93 in a Test Match.

A word about Mr. A. R. Abbit. He may not be a Bradman or a Larwood. He may play back to a half-volley, bowl the rankest of long hops, miss the easiest of "dollies." But he can be just as keen on the game, and enjoy it as much, as the first-class expert. One never knows. A moment of inspiration, a mighty swing, and wallop goes a six. A sudden, unexpected length ball, more by luck than judgment, and the century-maker wends his sad way back to the pavilion. An acrobatic leap and that "snorter" lands safely in his outstretched hand. Even if they never happen again, he will never forget the genuine thrill of those moments.

We had a foreign master at our school. Owing to illness, the staff were one short on the day of the annual Boys *v.* Masters match. He was persuaded to turn out. He came, weirdly and wonderfully arrayed. His brown and white shoes, purple socks, white pipe-line trouserings with blue stripes, silk shirt and flowing tie were a joy to behold. His turn came to bat. He entered. Standing fast-footed and firmly shutting his eyes, he swung his bat at the ball in a series of parabolas. He scored 30 in one over, including three sixes! His highest score since then has been a single, marred by seven chances. But, and it was twenty-five years ago, he still talks about that first innings.

One thinks of that band of lovers of cricket—the cricket writers. Though some of them may not have made their mark at the game, their love of it shines through their writings with a brilliant light. Neville Cardus, of the fascinating pen, the late Stewart Caine, Sidney Pardon, Sidney Southerton (all three Editors of *Wisden's Almanac*), to mention but a few. R. C. Robertson-Glasgow, whose bowling made Somerset feared, holds us with his compelling humour.

The late George Francis Wilson was a true cricket-lover. Owing to the kindness of his brother, Mr. J. S. Wilson, I am able to give you some of his thoughts.

On the googly:
>And, oh, to play the wizard by and by,
>>With rosy messenger to signify,
>And ever and anon with googlies strive
>>To wake new wonder in some batsman's eye!
>Who *waits* on googlies *him* shall they oppress:
>>They are not what they seem nor what you guess;
>They are of curly things the curliest,
>>Inviting least whom they would most possess.
>Approach, my friend, nor spread the secret far:
>>If you would wisely win the googlies' war,
>One step advance, pack prudence to the gate,
>>Then smite—as once they smote at Trafalgár.

Sound advice that!

On the yorker:

> Oh ye who ply for ever the straight bat,
>   And poke half-volleys and who off-balls pat;
> The fated YORKER is upon its way.
>   To bite the block and lay your middle flat.

A catch:

> That fielder's heart was conscious of the night
>   When first the stricken ball leapt into sight;
> That fielder's heart now simpler with delight
>   Sith in his hand he held the leather tight.

Memories of school days:

> Ye mighty batsmen of the M.C.C.
>   Confess ye know no more of ecstasy
> Than once ye knew, once when in academe,
>   You slogged your classics master for a three!

A close match:

> A shady seat at Lord's, an even score,
>   Nine wickets down, and only one ball more,
> With Jessop crouching, and with Trumble on——
>   And what were all golconda to a four!

A bad call:

> "Come!" cries the runner-up, and forward skips.
>   "Stay!" pleads the batsman, fearful of the slips.
> "Come!!" "Stay!!" Confused, two meet on one
>   man's ground,
>   "How's that!!!" and off the bails the bowler whips.

Puzzles are all the rage nowadays, so let us finish

off with one which, perhaps, you can explain. The persons in this little drama are as follows:

The Squire—a keen cricketer.

His daughter—beautiful, of course.

Jasper the villain—a fast bowler, dark and swarthy.

Gerald the hero—a golden-haired googly merchant.

The Village Schoolmaster—the scorer and keeper of the averages. He acts the part of the fairy queen, though, perforce, somewhat heavily disguised.

Jasper and Gerald, naturally, both loved the Squire's daughter.

The Squire announced that he would give ten thousand pounds, and, incidentally, his daughter's hand, to the one who headed the bowling averages at the end of the season.

The last match came. Each had taken forty wickets for one hundred and twenty runs during the course of the season. The day was fine. The wicket hard. Jasper rubbed his hands, and smiled his oily smile. Gerald went into a corner and practised googlies. In the match Jasper was in fine fettle, and took five wickets for thirty runs. An average of six. Poor Gerald's googlies would not google, and he only took one wicket for ten runs. An average of ten. So everybody crowded round Jasper and congratulated him. Then up and spake the Schoolmaster: "We have not worked out the averages yet. A mere matter of form, of course, but —er—" The crowd laughed. Then a most extraordinary thing came to light.

Here are the Schoolmaster's figures:

		Average
During season	Jasper 40 wickets 120 runs	3
Last match ...	5 wickets 30 runs	6
Total ...	45 wickets 150 runs	

```
      45)150(3.33
         135
         ───
         150
         135
         ───
         150
         135
         ───
```

		Average
During season	Gerald 40 wickets 120 runs	3
Last match ...	1 wicket 10 runs	10
Total ...	41 wickets 130 runs	

```
      41)130(3.17   The winning average!
         123
         ───
          70
          41
          ──
         290
         287
         ───
```

So virtue was triumphant and Gerald won.

But can you explain it?

Now we must draw stumps, lock up the pavilion, and so home to a well-earned rest.

EXTRAS

A Few Words About Some of the Giants of the Game—Past, Present and Future

We will take one or two names out of the bag at random.

Alfred Mynn, a hundred and fifty years ago, was, in every way, a great man. He was a huge man of Kent (or was he a Kentish man?). He was the Bradman of his day, and was known for his kindness and generosity. After his death, a poet wrote of him:

> Lightly lie the turf upon thee,
> Noble, kindly Alfred Mynn.

Then there was the fiddler:

> John Small
> Makes bat and ball;
> Pitch a wicket,
> Play at cricket
> With any man in England.

In the latter half of last century, the gigantic frame of "The Doctor," W. G. Grace, loomed like a Colossus over the world of cricket. A first-class cricketer at the early age of fifteen, he weighed nearly twenty stone before he gave up the game fifty years later. His scores were, like himself, enormous, and the wickets he took legion.

In the Gloucestershire team with "W. G." was G. L. Jessop of the rustic smite, whose hitting was like a full-throated chorus.

Soon came Jack Hobbs, who scored 197 centuries, and whose batting can be likened to a perfect symphony in music.

Among the moderns, Don Bradman stands out. Convention means nothing to him. Marvellous footwork and a perfect eye allow him to do the things that others dare not.

Frank Woolley is the ideal left-hander. Tall, with a tremendous reach, he gets balls, which are short of a length to most batsmen, on the half-volley, and sends them running to the boundary with effortless ease induced by supreme timing. He seems just to tap a six.

Patsy Hendren is a little "giant." Never still, always cracking jokes, and hooking the ball off his left eye-brow, he is a great character.

The greatest pair of bowlers to-day are Clarence Grimmett and W. O'Reilly of Australia. Little Grimmett, with his slow, spinning stuff and wonderful length, "thinks 'em out." He must be near the end of his career now, though. O'Reilly, the tall schoolmaster, is the very essence of attack and aggression, varying his pace and making the ball do unaccountable things off the pitch.

There are many others, but this chance-chosen list will suffice.

Here is the point.

The Giants of the Future? That is where *you* come in. No one knows who they will be. But they will come from the ranks of your generation.

CLOSE OF PLAY

Mr. P. C. Barnes has Written Some Thoughts Upon Umpiring

These Must be Taken to Heart

A few words upon umpiring.

I am afraid it is not realized nearly enough by the younger generation, nay, by a good proportion of the elders, how important umpiring is, and the great responsibility an umpire has in controlling the game, which in the senior classes means being "on duty" six consecutive hours each day and for three consecutive days. Each umpire either end has to see everything that takes place. He must know every rule of cricket laid down by the M.C.C., with the various amendments and additional clauses that have been made, and even finds it necessary at times to refer to the M.C.C. an incident which has occurred in a match and which is not covered by any existing rule.

It has been found in the past that some of us, when we feel that our "playing powers" have gone, take up umpiring, which by many cricketers is considered the next best thing to playing. If any readers do take up umpiring, do please bear in mind the following few *golden rules*:

(1) First and foremost, you must be *fair*. If you are biased in the slightest degree, *pack up*.

(2) Thoroughly study the Laws of Cricket—there are over fifty of them; and do not attempt to officiate until you are definitely sure that you know them.

(3) In making decisions, be firm and definite, and never give them in a hesitating way—you are always assisted by the sound law: "If you are not able to decide upon an appeal, you may refer to your colleague the other end."

(4) Always use the given signs. Give them clearly and see that they are acknowledged by the scorers.

(5) Should your decision to an appeal be unfavourably met with by a batsman—this should never be—repeat your decision pleasantly, and *give no sign* of making an inquest.

(6) Remember always you are umpiring with your side and not for it.

(7) Remember you are the "key man." A game cannot be played without you.